Agricultural Development of Taiwan
1903–1960

Agricultural Development of Taiwan 1903–1960

YHI-MIN HO

Vanderbilt University Press
1966

To My Wife

ACKNOWLEDGMENTS

I am deeply indebted to Professor Anthony M. Tang of Vanderbilt University for his wise counsel during the preparation of the book. It is much the better for his many inspiring criticisms and suggestions. I am also grateful to Professor T. W. Schultz of the University of Chicago, who took his invaluable time to read through the manuscript and made a number of suggestions, to Professor Rudolph C. Blitz of Vanderbilt University, who helped me the similar manner in making suggestions and offering criticisms, and to Professor Donald L. Huddle of Rice University, who read the manuscript at the early draft stage. Messrs Frank J. H. Ma, Tzuo-Yuan Wang, and Yaw-Chin Ho and many others extended their generous assistance to me in collecting data and literally made the study possible. To them, I am indeed thankful. Thanks are due the Vanderbilt University Press for making the publication possible and to Miss Elizabeth Chase, Assistant Editor of the Press, for her efficient and skillful editing. Finally, I would like to express my appreciation of the encouragement and understanding of my wife and of her help in preparing the manuscript in many ways.

October 1966

YHI-MIN HO

CONTENTS

TABLES

Agricultural Development of Taiwan
1903–1960

Chapter 1

INTRODUCTION

The rapidly growing economic development literature has produced a certain consensus on developmental strategies for underdeveloped countries, but it has also demonstrated the undisputable fact that economists have failed so far to develop a theory for development. There is no comprehensive and acceptable explanation of why some countries at one time or another have emerged into and sustained the cumulative growth process while others have failed. Indeed, until economists can identify the leading force or forces of growth, economic planning in underdeveloped countries will be largely a matter of planners' personal preferences. It is rather confusing to find in the literature all possible factors and forces, economic or noneconomic, that are immediately identified as characteristics of an underdeveloped economy and regarded as relevant and essential to the problem. Although a large number of those identified factors or conditions may be the effects rather than the causes of underdevelopment and consequently are irrelevant from the point of view of remedy, the process of identifying has brought economists closer to the core of the issue, i.e., the arrangement of development priorities. Priorities must be arranged because no underdeveloped country can attack on every front simultaneously the problem of underdevelopment. The practical aspect of the problem is then a matter of finding the optimal allocation of resources which will lead to a maximum rate of growth consistent with a society's welfare function.

One of the contemporary controversies over development priority is the problem of agricultural versus industrial development. Those who observe the continual decline of the importance of agriculture in the process of economic development and the relatively small part played by agriculture in advanced economies associate poverty with agriculture. According to this point of view the problem of economic development is then largely a matter of how to transform the structure of an economy. In other words, economic development is considered to be identical to industrialization. This viewpoint apparently disregards completely the role of agriculture and overlooks possible contributions of agriculture to economic development. Presenting the opposite point of view, Jacob Viner argues,

. . . the real problem in poor countries is not agriculture as such, or the absence of manufacture as such, but poverty and backwardness, poor agriculture, or poor agriculture and poor manufacture. The real remedy is to remove the basic causes of poverty and backwardness.[1]

Professor William H. Nicholls stresses the fact, based on the experience in England and other advanced countries, that either the industrial revolution had been preceded by an agricultural revolution or there had to be a substantial agricultural surplus before mass industrialization was begun.[2] He then argues that until underdeveloped countries succeed in achieving and sustaining a reliable food surplus (either through domestic production or imports), they have not fulfilled the fundamental precondition for economic development.[3] Professor Nicholas Kaldor takes the same position by saying that

. . . economic development will of course invariably involve industrialization (or at any rate the relative growth of secondary and tertiary industries taken together) but this can be expected to follow, almost automatically upon the growth of the food surplus of the agricultural sector . . . whereas it is certainly not the case a rise in industrial production in itself induces greater agricultural supplies. Once this is recognized, the efforts of underdeveloped countries (should) be concentrated . . . far more than they are at present . . . on tackling the problem of how to raise productivity on the land as a prior condition of industrial development.[4]

Although recognizing the important role agriculture must play in

1. *International Trade and Economic Development,* p. 71.
2. "The Place of Agriculture in Economic Development," a paper presented at a Round Table on Economic Development with particular reference to East Asia (sponsored by the International Economic Association), and "An 'Agricultural Surplus' as a Factor in Economic Development," *Journal of Political Economy,* LXXI, No. 1 (February 1963), 1–29. A rise in agricultural productivity and the existence of an agricultural surplus may not be the same thing. Historically, however, the emergence of an agricultural surplus has often been accompanied by an increase in agricultural productivity, especially if a minimum biological subsistent level is assumed.
3. Simon Kuznets reaches the same conclusion of considering a marked rise in productivity per worker in agriculture a precondition of the industrial revolution in any part of the world. See Simon Kuznets, *Six Lectures on Economic Growth,* pp. 59–60. That "it takes more than industry to industrialize" represents the same line of argument. See Walter W. Rostow, *The Stages of Economic Growth,* pp. 22–24.
4. *Essays on Economic Stability and Growth,* p. 242.

economic development, the so-called "balanced-growth" theorists, led by W. Arthur Lewis, view the matter somewhat differently. In one respect, balanced-growth theorists stress the importance of keeping development of one sector of an economy in step with other sectors. The industrial sector should not be developed too far ahead of agriculture or vice versa. A certain proportion is to be maintained in line with demand elasticities so that the development process can proceed smoothly. Lewis even declares that "the secret of most development problems is to maintain a proper balance between sectors." [5] In Lewis's two-sector model, agriculture has two distinctive roles. Growth in agricultural output consistent with the expansion of the nonagricultural sector is necessary to maintain stable terms of trade between the two sectors.[6] Failure in bringing about an increase in the supply of agricultural output either will cause prices of food products to rise or imports of food products to become necessary; either one will be deflationary on the nonagricultural sector. Conversely, deteriorating terms of trade against agriculture adversely affect farmers' real income and, unless foreign markets are established, the demand for nonagricultural products. Logically, he asserts that "smooth economic development requires that industry and agriculture should grow together." [7] Understandably, Lewis is critical of economists from the industrial countries who urge agricultural countries to concentrate upon agriculture and do nothing to advance their industry.[8] On the other hand, he attacks those economists who take the exact opposite position by identifying economic development with industrialization.[9]

The theory of balanced growth in its narrower form has been transformed into the "big-push" theory, whose foundation rests on the indivis-

5. W. Arthur Lewis, *The Theory of Economic Growth,* p. 141.

6. A stable terms of trade may be maintained through a concurrent expansion of industry and agriculture in line with demand elasticities, and the expansion of a nonagricultural sector may come to a halt through the effect on industrial wages of the improved productivity of the subsistence sector in Lewis's two-sector model. Lewis, "Economic Development with Unlimited Supply of Labour," *The Manchester School.* May 1954, reprinted in A. N. Agarwala and S. P. Singh, *The Economics of Underdevelopment.* Lewis's two-sector model is highly simplified; for the refined Lewis's two-sector model, see Gustav Ranis and J. C. H. Fei, "A Theory of Economic Development," *American Economic Review,* LI (September 1961), 553–565.

7. Lewis, *Theory of Economic Growth,* p. 227.

8. *Ibid.,* p. 283.

9. *Ibid.*

ibility of investment, demand, and saving.[10] The principal implication of the theory expounded by Rosenstein-Rodan is vividly summarized in an often-cited passage: "There is a minimum level of resource that must be devoted to . . . a development program."[11] Nurkse's shoe factory has also become a classical example of the relevance of this theory. In order to get development underway, according to the "big-push" theory, a large number of industries must be started simultaneously. This theory has merit in principle but not in reality.[12] A country would never have been classified as underdeveloped if it had the resources available to launch an effective push on all fronts.

In applying the "big-push" doctrine to agriculture, Benjamin Higgins suggested, "as for a wholesale shift to mechanized commercial agriculture, it is not an operation to be carried out on a piecemeal private enterprise basis."[13] He believes, "only a unified and large-scale program involving more rapid industrialization and bold scheme for agricultural improvement can launch cumulative growth."[14] He reached this conclusion on the belief that in densely populated, underdeveloped countries marginal productivities of both labor and capital are close to zero in the rural sector. To raise the marginal productivity of capital in agriculture it is necessary to greatly increase the ratio of land to labor. The size of farms must be increased, for example, from 2 or 3 acres to 20 or 200 acres so that mechanization becomes practical and profitable. The consolidation of land-holding of such vast extent requires a large-scale industrial expansion to absorb displaced agricultural population. Apparently,

. . . it requires heavy investment in both industrial and agricultural sectors. Neither agricultural improvements on the present holdings nor industrialization will, by itself, break through this particular vicious circle.[15]

10. P. N. Rosenstein-Rodan, "Problems of Industrialization of Eastern and South-Eastern Europe," *Economic Journal,* LIII (June–September 1943), 202–211, and "Notes on the Theory of the 'Big-Push,' " (Center for International Studies, Massachusetts Institute of Technology), and Ragner Nurkse, *Problems of Capital Formation in Underdeveloped Countries,* ch. 1.

11. Rosenstein-Rodan, "Notes on the Theory," p. 1.

12. See for example Marcus Fleming, "External Economies and the Doctrines of Balanced Growth," reprinted in Agarwala and Singh, *The Economics of Underdevelopment.* See also Albert O. Hirschman, *The Strategy of Economic Development.*

13. *Economic Development: Problems, Principles, and Policies,* p. 344.

14. *Ibid.*

15. *Ibid.,* p. 343.

In comparison with Higgins, Lewis asserts that the consequences of present small farm holdings in densely populated, underdeveloped countries can be overcome by investment in agriculture. He believes that

> . . . when agriculture is in the hands of small farmers, the introduction of innovation depends more upon government initiative than upon the initiative of private entrepreneurs.[16]

Farm output can be increased through considerable expenditure on roads, rural water supplies, agricultural credit facilities, and other services, which are essentially in the government sphere.

One of the characteristics of an underdeveloped economy is the high ratio of agricultural labor force to the total labor force. The sharpest contrast between a developed and an underdeveloped country lies in the tremendous discrepancy of labor productivities in agriculture. Unless labor productivity in agriculture can be substantially raised, it is very unlikely that development of an undeveloped economy can proceed into self-sustained and cumulative growth. Economic development can be sustained only when a substantial improvement in agriculture has been achieved. Industrialization generates certain dynamic forces which bring about changes away from the traditional structure of underdeveloped countries. It is equally true that "a neglect of policies promoting increased agricultural productivity may have serious repercussion on the rate of general economic progress."[17] The experience of Soviet Russia is a case in point. Economists who associate economic development with industrialization could have learned a good lesson from Russia's difficulty with her agricultural production.[18] For most contemporary underdeveloped countries, industrialization without an agricultural revolution would merely underscore their present difficulties.[19] An efficient agricultural sector and a sufficiently large agricultural surplus can contribute to general economic development in the following ways: (1) by meeting substantial increases in the demand for food as the low-income countries experience growth (failure to do so undermines industrialization through terms of trade changes or competing demand on

16. Lewis, *Theory of Economic Growth*, p. 279.

17. Nicholls, "The Place of Agriculture," p. 13.

18. When Russia started her mass industrialization, she had an impressive agricultural surplus that most contemporary underdeveloped countries do not possess.

19. Higgins, *op. cit.*, p. 343.

foreign exchanges occasioned by food imports); (2) by permitting expansion of exports of agricultural products (one of the most promising means of increasing income and foreign exchange earnings, particularly in the earlier stage of development); (3) by freeing labor for employment in manufacturing and other expanding sectors; (4) by contributing to the capital required for overhead investment and expansion of secondary industry; (5) by raising real income of the farm population to stimulate industrial expansion; and (6) by developing talents and attitudes favorable to development.[20]

Although agricultural improvement is essential to general economic development, agricultural improvement or a substantial food surplus is not the fundamental precondition for economic development. It is quite conceivable that agricultural improvement can proceed more smoothly if it is incorporated with industrial development in an integrated developmental scheme. Agriculture's contribution to economic growth will not be enhanced if agricultural improvement precedes general economic development, nor will it be hampered if agricultural development proceeds side by side with industrial development. This precondition argument is apt to be thought of as an antithesis to the fundamentalist argument for industrialization. It is conceivable that any kind of surplus that an underdeveloped country possesses can be utilized to finance economic development. Why then is an agricultural surplus singled out as the fundamental precondition instead of some other surplus? An agricultural revolution did precede the industrial revolution in England and other Western European countries, but in the case of Japan, "the agricultural revolution . . . though not in the sense of the Western type was proceeding side by side with her industrial expansion." [21] It is very likely that Japan's experience in developing her economy may be more relevant to the contemporary underdeveloped countries than the experience of England and other advanced countries.

Current controversy over agricultural versus industrial development is equally vague if not also misleading. True, agricultural and industrial developments are competing in using resources. They are also comple-

20. Bruce F. Johnston and John W. Mellor, "The Role of Agriculture in Economic Development," *American Economic Review,* LI (September 1961), pp. 571–581. See also Nicholls, "The Place of Agriculture."
21. K. Ohkawa and H. Rosovsky, "The Role of Agriculture in Modern Japanese Economic Development," *Economic Development and Cultural Change,* LX, No. 1, Pt. II (October 1960), 43–67.

mentary in many important ways. Once the importance to general economic development of an efficient agriculture is recognized, the relevant and crucial question to ask then is whether the competitive aspect of the concurrent development of agriculture and industry can be reduced or, if possible, avoided. This depends on how agricultural development can be obtained and sustained. If one considers that agricultural growth can be obtained only through a bold scheme of wholesale mechanization and large-scale land consolidation, as Higgins has suggested, the competitive character takes on greater substance and one is forced to accept either of two positions: (1) the balanced "big-push" doctrines or (2) taking either side in the agriculture versus industry controversy. Large-scale mechanization and other "big-push" approaches may indeed transform traditional, low-productivity agriculture in underdeveloped countries into modern and productive agriculture. However, the resources required to carry out such a policy must be well beyond the reach of all underdeveloped countries, particularly since additional resources are needed to expand the industrial sector to absorb the displaced agricultural population. Do developing countries have any other alternative within the limit of their resources?

Professor T. W. Schultz believes

. . . there is a logical economic basis why traditional agriculture employing only the factors of production at its disposal is incapable of growth except at high cost, and why the rate of return to investment in modern agricultural factors can be high by past growth standards. Thus it really does matter what is done in developing agriculture in countries that want to achieve economic growth as cheaply as possible.[22]

He further asserts

. . . rapid sustained growth rests heavily on particular investments in farm people related to the new skills and new knowledge that farm people must acquire to succeed at the game of growth from agriculture.[23]

Agriculture in contemporary underdeveloped countries is characterized by the attributes of Schultz's traditional agriculture, in which production is based wholly on traditional and conventional factors of production. As the state of the arts and the state of preferences and motives to acquire additional income in the traditional agriculture have

22. *Transforming Traditional Agriculture*, p. 5.
23. *Ibid.*, p. 177.

remained long enough, marginal productivity of capital and net savings approach zero. Lack of incentive to save and invest is the logical outcome of the economic relationship of cost and return instead of a phenomenom to be explained in terms of cultural differences, as some economists are inclined to believe. Traditional agriculture is far less productive in comparison with a modern agriculture, but it is efficient in utilizing all factors at its disposal. Agricultural improvement through reallocation of the existing, traditional factors and through increases in the stock of such factors is expensive and offers only limited scope. Therefore, according to Schultz, the transformation of traditional agriculture lies in the supply of new and nonconventional farm inputs and the skills of farm people in using them effectively. Investment in human agents in agriculture, Schultz asserts, is the key to a rapid growth from agriculture. And human capital in agriculture constitutes the major and cheapest source of growth.

If nonconventional farm inputs can be effectively applied on small as well as on large farms, then a technical revolution becomes feasible and attainable without a heavy draw on scarce resources and without a parallel social revolution involving large-scale consolidation of land holdings to transform traditional agriculture.[24] In contrast with mass mechanization of agriculture and other grandeur schemes, technical revolution in agriculture through the introduction of new farm inputs of land-saving and labor-intensive character requires few scarce resources. From this point of view, concurrent development of agriculture and industry is not only desirable but economically feasible. Consequently, the real issue involved here is not an uncompromising choice between industrial or agricultural development. As Professor Anthony M. Tang rightly points out, the real issue is:

> What is the most efficacious way of obtaining a high rate of industrialization given the resources and income constraints of the underdeveloped countries? If agricultural output can be augmented largely by means containing little or no opportunity costs, then agricultural development complements and hastens industrial development.[25]

24. Agriculture in underdeveloped countries is of low productivity regardless of the size of farm operation.
25. "Agriculture and Economic Development in Underdeveloped Countries with Particular Reference to Mainland China," Economics Department, Vanderbilt University, 1961, p. 7.

Although the idea of a parallel development between industry and agriculture is similar to Lewis's balanced growth theory, it differs in one important aspect. In Lewis's balanced growth model, an appropriate rate of growth is maintained to keep agriculture and industry in balance; this is determined by the country's marginal propensity to consume agricultural products compared with the marginal propensity to consume manufactured goods. Instead of maintaining a rigid balance, the idea of parallel development is aimed at attaining the highest possible overall rate of growth within the restraint of resources available. Any imbalance that may result is implicitly viewed as a problem to be solved through trade.

The successful experience of Japan in her agricultural development has become a classical example often cited in current development literature.[26] Throughout the sixty-year period from 1881 to 1940, Japan doubled the production of her six major crops principally as a consequence of the increase of crop yields. The area devoted to crops increased only 18 percent, whereas yields rose 66 percent.[27] The development and use of improved seeds, increased application of chemical fertilizers, improvements in farm practice, pest control, and progess in irrigation systems were important factors in the increase in crop yields. Japan's methods of developing her agriculture have the following merits and features: (1) they are land-saving and labor-intensive devices suitable for high labor-to-land ratio condition in agriculture, (2) they can be effectively applied to small farms, and (3) capital outlays required are small.[28] The most significant aspect of the Japanese case is that it dramatically illustrates how agricultural improvement can be accomplished by investing in the human agent in agriculture without drawing scarce resources of an economy. As Schultz points out,

. . . the modern complex pattern of production activities that characterizes Japanese agriculture has been made possible by two types of public invest-

26. See for example (1) Lewis, *Theory of Economic Growth,* ch. 5; (2) Bruce F. Johnston, "Agricultural Productivity and Economic Development in Japan," *Journal of Political Economy,* LIX (December 1951), 498–513; (3) Nicholls, "The Place of Agriculture"; (4) Ohkawa and Rosovsky, "The Role of Agriculture"; and (5) Bruce F. Johnston, "Agricultural Development and Economic Transformation: Japan, Taiwan, and Denmark," a paper presented for the Conference on Relations between Agriculture and Economic Growth (November 1960).
27. Johnston, "Agricultural Development," p. 27.
28. Johnston, "Agricultural Productivity."

ments: (1) investment in research to discover and develop agricultural fac-ors specifically tailored to the biological and other requirements of Japan, and (2) investment in schooling not only of a corps of specialists to extend this knowledge to farm people but of farm people themselves, which among other things has enhanced their abilities successfully to employ these new inputs which involve complex and difficult farm practices.[29]

The return to this type of investment in Japan is indeed impressive. According to Tang's estimates, investment in rural education and agricultural research produced a rate of return of 35 percent.[30] It is conceivable that Japan's method of developing her agriculture can be equally applied to other regions with similar land and labor conditions.

The Japanese experience is not unique. The growth of Taiwan's agricultural sector from 1901 to 1960 is another interesting and revealing case in which human capital played a vital role. During this period, Taiwan achieved very impressive progress in its agricultural production. Gross agricultural output measured by 1952–1956 farm prices increased sixfold, whereas land input and labor input rose only twofold and 50 percent, respectively. Apparently, gains in factor productivity account for a large portion of the increment in farm output. It is estimated that productivity of aggregate input (land, labor, capital) gained by 60 percent; land productivity, by 180 percent; labor productivity, by 230 percent; and productivity of fixed capital, by 215 percent. Gains in factor productivity during the course of Taiwan's agricultural development take two concrete forms: (1) changes in the degree of land utilization, and (2) increases in the yields from each unit of land input. The appearance of new, nonconventional farm inputs and the skills of farm people in utilizing them effectively are found to be the major source of Taiwan's agricultural growth. Varietal improvement in seeds characterized by greater yields and shorter growing periods, increased and improved application of fertilizers (both chemical and domestic), improvement in farming methods, improved crop rotational systems, and the provision of irrigation facilities are the proximate causes and factors. The underlying factors of the phenomenal gains in agricultural productivity are investment activities in agricultural research and rural

29. Schultz, *op. cit.,* p. 190.
30. Anthony M. Tang, "Research and Education in Japanese Agricultural Development, 1880–1938," *Economic Studies Quarterly,* XIII (Part I: February 1963; Part II: May 1963), pp. 27–41, 91–99.

education. The estimated social return to investment of this type in Taiwan gives a marginal efficiency as high as 55 percent.

The pattern of Taiwan's agricultural development in many important aspects is similar to the Japanese experience. One can actually regard the case of Taiwan as the first successful experience of transplanting the Japanese developmental methods to another region. The experience in both cases constitutes historical examples of agricultural growth without drawing upon the scarce resources of an economy and illustrates the importance of investment activities in the human agent for a rapid and sustained growth in agriculture. In both cases, provision of irrigation and chemical fertilizers occupied an important place in the transformation of agriculture. However, as one will see in later chapters in this study, the sustained growth of Taiwan's agriculture rests on the continual infusion of new farm inputs. Investment in irrigation and fertilizer plants becomes attractive and rewarding only when yield-increasing forms of investment take place simultaneously or successively. It is also significant that in both cases the rapid and sustained growth of agriculture has been accomplished under unfavorable land-to-labor conditions.

The purpose of this study is to analyze the sources and pattern of Taiwan's successful agricultural transformation from 1901 to 1960 and to illustrate the role of land-saving and labor-intensive nonconventional farm inputs in agricultural development under a small farm-holding system. More specifically, the study takes on the following tasks: (1) measuring Taiwan's long-term growth in agricultural output as well as changes in input combinations and in factor productivity; (2) estimating from statistics output increases resulting from the accumulation of conventional inputs as well as the residual attributable to other factors; and (3) identifying factors that are responsible for the residual.

This book is divided into ten chapters. The nature of Taiwan's agricultural production statistics, methods of estimating and constructing the output index, changes in the output component, and the growth rates of Taiwan's farm output from 1901 to 1960 will be discussed and presented in Chapters Two and Three. Chapters Four and Five are devoted to a discussion and analysis of Taiwan's agricultural employment, fixed capital and working capital in agriculture, and farm land. The method of constructing the input index and long-term changes in factor productivities are contained in Chapter Six. Identification of factors responsible for the computed residuals and measurement of income flows from these sources are treated in Chapters Eight, Nine, and Ten.

The scope of this study is delimited geographically to include Taiwan proper and Penghu Islands (also known as the Pescadores). Kingment (Quemoy) and Matsu are excluded. The study covers the period from 1901 to 1960 because no reliable data are available before 1901. The term *agriculture* used in this book excludes forestry and fishery.

THE NATURE OF TAIWAN'S OUTPUT DATA AND THE CONSTRUCTION OF THE OUTPUT INDEX

A study of long-term change in agricultural production calls for the measurement of changes in agricultural output and agricultural input over time. Conventionally changes are measured by the construction of an input index and an output index. It is a simple matter to obtain an output index if two parallel series are available, namely: (1) physical amount of agricultural products produced and (2) their prices. An output index can be calculated by using the following formula:

$$Q = \Sigma Q_n P_n / \Sigma Q_0 P_0$$

$$N = 1, 2, 3, \ldots n$$

In the formula Q_0 stands for the physical quantities and P_0 for the prices of the base period, Q_n stands for the physical quantities and P_n for the prices of any period that is to be compared. However, the output index so obtained contains price changes as well as changes in physical products produced. Price changes have to be removed before meaningful comparisons in real terms can be made. Therefore, either a Laspeyres's or a Paasche's price index can be used to deflate the series calculated from the above formula. If a Laspeyres's price index is used as the deflator, the result is a Paasche's quantity index:

$$\frac{\Sigma Q_n P_n}{\Sigma Q_0 P_0} \Big/ \frac{\Sigma P_n Q_0}{\Sigma P_0 Q_0} = \frac{\Sigma Q_n P_n}{\Sigma Q_0 P_n}$$

If a Paasche's price index is used as the deflator, the result is a Laspeyres's quantity index:

$$\frac{\Sigma Q_n P_n}{\Sigma Q_0 P_0} \Big/ \frac{\Sigma P_n Q_n}{\Sigma P_0 Q_n} = \frac{\Sigma P_0 Q_n}{\Sigma P_0 Q_0}$$

When the output series in monetary terms and/or a consistent price index are missing, the task of constructing an output series in real terms is complicated. Unfortunately, this is exactly the case in Taiwan. No single consistent price index exists which covers the entire period from 1901 to 1960; values of agricultural products series for the years between 1901 and 1944 are scattered and incomplete and are recorded in terms of (old) Taiwan dollars, a local currency used during the short period between 1946–49.[1] Since both the price index and the value of agricultural output series are missing, neither a Laspayres's quantity index nor a Paasche's quantity index can be constructed in the manner shown above. However, physical quantities of agricultural products produced are known since 1922 and data of major agricultural products are available back to 1896. A feasible alternative then is to aggregate the physical quantities of various agricultural products by using the known farm prices of a particular period as weights. The calculation of the quantity index takes this familiar form:

$$\Sigma \ Q_n P' / \Sigma \ Q_0 P'$$

The output index as shown in Table 1 and Figure 1 is derived according to the above formula with the 1952–1956 average farm prices used as weights.

A total of 74 different products, including 15 food crops, 7 special crops, 24 items of vegetables, 19 items of fruits, and 4 livestock and poultry products, are covered in the output index shown. The index as compiled covers about 90 percent of Taiwan's farm output. The coverage of the index is higher for the earlier years of the period than for the later years. However, no correction is made since the coverage of individual crop statistics is assumed to be the same throughout the period.

The validity of the method adopted and, consequently, the quality of the index depend on the implicit and crucial assumption that the relative price structure of agricultural products during the base period chosen is truly representative of the whole period. In an attempt to find the extent to which the change in relative prices might affect the index, output indices for a number of other base weight periods are constructed

---

1. All value series were undoubtedly distorted to a great extent because they are originally recorded in Japanese yen and later converted into (old) Taiwan dollars. Taiwan was under the Japanese rule from 1895 to 1945.

TABLE 1

Index of Agricultural Output,
1901–1960

Year	Index	Five-Year Moving Average
1901	100.00	
1902	101.08	
1903	130.04	126.11
1904	145.57	135.72
1905	153.84	147.67
1906	148.07	155.48
1907	160.85	160.82
1908	169.07	163.67
1909	172.26	169.58
1910	168.11	169.37
1911	177.60	171.91
1912	159.80	172.27
1913	181.78	176.35
1914	174.06	180.40
1915	188.49	191.49
1916	197.85	195.79
1917	215.29	202.18
1918	203.28	202.75
1919	205.98	203.42
1920	191.36	205.45
1921	201.21	208.65
1922	225.42	218.91
1923	219.27	235.01
1924	257.31	248.12
1925	271.82	259.38
1926	266.78	274.30
1927	281.74	281.91
1928	293.87	290.80
1929	295.33	302.12
1930	316.28	219.92
1931	323.40	327.91
1932	370.70	341.64
1933	333.86	356.48
1934	363.94	372.95
1935	390.51	381.03
1936	405.75	400.39
1937	411.41	414.58
1938	430.63	411.35
1939	434.91	404.05
1940	374.37	396.61

TABLE 1 (Continued)

Year	Index	Five-Year Moving Average
1941	369.22	381.97
1942	374.24	355.26
1943	357.42	316.51
1944	301.34	284.17
1945	180.62	259.31
1946	207.52	247.27
1947	249.99	256.31
1948	297.19	298.56
1949	346.52	337.83
1950	391.90	376.09
1951	403.85	415.92
1952	441.27	446.28
1953	496.38	467.19
1954	498.29	494.51
1955	496.44	523.94
1956	540.47	459.46
1957	588.44	573.65
1958	623.95	598.31
1959	619.23	
1960	619.74	

Source: See the text.

with one taking 1956–1960 average farm prices as weights. As shown in Table 2, the two indices are very close. True, the two base periods chosen are not far apart; consequently, one does not expect the two to be greatly different. Still there are reasons to believe that changes in relative prices during the period were relatively insignificant. S. C. Hsieh and T. H. Lee of the Chinese-American Joint Commission on Rural Reconstruction, Taiwan, compiled an output index based on 1935–1937 prices of Taiwan's agriculture. Again the two indices are very close. For detailed comparison, see the last section of this chapter.

In measuring long-term change in agricultural production, three different but related concepts are relevant and can be employed: (1) gross agricultural production, (2) gross agricultural output, and (3) net agricultural output. Gross agricultural production has a much broader scope than the other two, as it includes those agricultural products (e.g., seeds and feeds) used on farms as intermediate products. Gross agricultural output is exclusive of the part of agricultural products

Figure 1

INDEX OF AGRICULTURAL OUTPUT

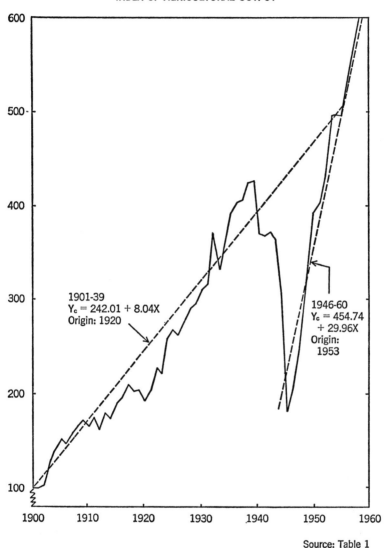

1901-39
$Y_c = 242.01 + 8.04X$
Origin: 1920

1946-60
$Y_c = 454.74 + 29.96X$
Origin: 1953

Source: Table 1

used on farms as intermediate products. Net agricultural output differs from gross agricultural output in that it is the remainder after the subtraction of all production expenses incurred, e.g., expenses on fertilizers, depreciation of farm implements, equipment and farm build-

TABLE 2

Output Index for Selected Years

1901 = 100

	1910	1920	1930	1940	1950	1960
Output index (1952–1956 prices)	168.11	191.36	316.28	374.37	391.90	619.74
Output index (1956–1960 prices)	165.53	188.51	312.36	369.67	384.67	617.69

Source: See Table 1.

ings, and irrigation fees.[2] Which concept is more appropriate in measuring changes in agricultural production over a long period of time? If the portion of the farm crops, dairy products, and livestock used on farms as intermediate products is a constant proportion of the gross agricultural production, an index based on gross agricultural production will be identical with the index based on gross agricultural output. Frequently this may not be the case. If this portion changes over time, the index of gross agricultural production will be either an overstatement or an understatement as far as the contribution of agriculture to total output is concerned. The output index constructed here is based on gross agricultural output because gross agricultural production figures contain double counting whereas net farm output is more relevant when consideration is to be given to changes in farm income over time.[3]

As stated above, the index is calculated by aggregating the physical output of 74 agricultural products, each weighted by the 1952–1956 average farm prices. Data on gross agricultural output are not available; only gross production data were recorded for all crops. Estimates have to be made to derive output figures from gross production for each

2. Theoretically, the depreciation of farm houses can be separated into two parts—one part assignable to production and the other part to consumption. Actually, in Taiwan and other less developed regions, dwellings and service buildings are frequently inseparable.

3. Gross output tends to exaggerate the contribution of agriculture as agricultural inputs drawn from the nonagricultural sector increase over time. The value-added concept is not applied in this study because the data are not available.

individual crop. Ralph N. Gleason made estimates of the portions of different agricultural products retained and used on farms as seeds and feeds in *Taiwan Food Balances: 1935–1954*. His coefficients of estimation are adopted here and used to estimate farm products retained and used on farms as seeds and feeds for the whole period from 1901 to 1960. Gross farm output series are obtained by subtracting seeds and feeds so calculated from gross production figures of each individual crop. The detailed process is described in Appendix A. For a number of crops, even gross production data are not available for the earlier years. Estimates then are made to fill the gap; the detail is discussed in the following section.

Gross agricultural production data are taken from the following five sources:

The Statistical Summary of Taiwan for the Past 51 Years, compiled by the Statistical Bureau, Taiwan Provincial Government in 1946

Taiwan Agricultural Statistics: 1901–1955, compiled in 1956 by the Chinese American Joint Commission on Rural Reconstruction (English version)

Taiwan Food Statistics, published annually by the Food Bureau of Taiwan Provincial Government

Taiwan Agricultural Yearbook, Department of Agriculture and Forestry, Taiwan Provincial Government

Taiwan Statistical Abstract, an annual publication of the Bureau of Accounting and Statistics, Taiwan Provincial Government.

Statistical Summary is the most comprehensive statistical record for the years between 1901 and 1944; *Taiwan Agricultural Statistics: 1901–1955* is actually a supplement to that publication and covers an additional eleven years. Excepting minor discrepancies, data recorded in both volumes are extremely consistent.[4] For this reason, they all retain the same deficiency in incompleteness of data for a number of products for the earlier years. *Taiwan Agricultural Yearbook* contains reliable and complete information of agricultural production for the postwar

---

4. The discrepancy is found in the case of rice production for the period from 1937 to 1945. Since the data recorded in *Taiwan Agricultural Statistics* are inconsistent themselves, production figures recorded in *The Statistical Summary* are adopted here. Joint Commission on Rural Reconstruction, *Taiwan Agricultural Statistics: 1901–1955* and Taiwan, Department of Statistics, *Statistical Summary of Taiwan for the Past 51 Years.*

period only. Food crop statistics are compiled in *Taiwan Food Statistics*. *Taiwan Statistical Abstract* contains only production of major crops for the postwar period.

To facilitate the discussion of the nature of data of individual crops, all crops are classified into six categories—food and common crops, special crops, fiber crops, vegetables, fruits, and livestock and poultry products.

1. Food and common crops. Of the fifteen different crops covered in this category, data of all but Indian corn and arrow root are available since 1901; physical quantities of Indian corn produced are known since 1927; of arrow root since 1918. Production of sorghum was included in barnyard millet until 1937. Production of soybeans are separated from "other beans" since 1913.[5]

2. Special crops. Among the seven special crops, citronella plant, coffee, perfume plants, and derris are relatively new crops to Taiwan. Their production data are available since the mid-1930s. The other three crops—sugar cane, tea and tobacco—are major cash crops of Taiwan of which production data are complete since 1901.[6]

3. Fiber crops. Data on all but sisal and cotton are available since 1901. Data on sisal production are available only from 1940 and cotton from 1935. The two crops were introduced to Taiwan in the 1930s.

4. Vegetable crops. Complete data on vegetable production were not recorded until 1918. Data on potatoes, scallion, other root vegetables, stem vegetables, Chinese cabbage, water convolvulus, celery, other leaf and flower vegetables, kidney beans, oriental pickling melons, wax-gourd, and other fruit vegetables appear after 1918. Estimates are made for individual crops back to 1918 as well as for vegetable crops as a group for the period from 1901 to 1917 (for detail, see Appendix A).

5. Fruits. The nature of data of fruit production is the same as for vegetables except most fruit production data are available since 1909.

6. Livestock and poultry products. Data of livestock slaughtered and number of poultry are missing for 1904–1906, and data of total weights of livestock slaughtered are lacking for the period of 1901–

5. *Statistical Summary*, Table 205, pp. 556–557.
6. Sugar cane production data are missing for 1901; the estimation is based on sugar exports of the year.

1910. Estimates have to be made. (For detail, also see Appendix A.)
The complete output series compiled for the period under review is shown in Table 3.

The agricultural output index compiled by Hsieh and Lee of the Chinese-American Joint Commission on Rural Reconstruction consists

TABLE 3

Gross Agricultural Output, 1901–1960

(In 1952–1956 average prices)
Unit: NT$1,000,000

Year	Total	Food Crop	Special Crop	Fiber Crop	Vege-tables [a]	Fruits [b]	Livestock & Poultry
1901	1,506.9	1,092.3	138.3	7.7	36.7	39.6	192.3
1902	1,523.2	1,020.5	179.0	11.5	37.1	40.0	235.1
1903	1,959.6	1,398.9	147.7	18.7	47.8	51.5	295.0
1904	2,193.6	1,607.6	150.0	20.0	53.5	57.7	304.6
1905	2,318.3	1,629.0	232.0	18.2	56.5	60.9	321.7
1906	2,231.3	1,511.1	262.0	22.7	54.4	58.7	322.4
1907	2,423.9	1,701.4	245.6	23.6	59.1	63.7	330.5
1908	2,547.7	1,798.0	250.0	16.1	62.1	67.0	354.5
1909	2,595.8	1,771.1	310.6	18.2	63.3	61.1	371.5
1910	2,533.3	1,571.6	410.4	13.4	61.8	76.6	399.5
1911	2,676.2	1,670.7	494.4	14.1	65.3	65.0	366.7
1912	2,408.0	1,503.6	372.8	15.4	58.7	57.3	400.2
1913	2,739.2	1,927.3	263.3	16.4	66.8	52.2	413.2
1914	2,622.9	1,739.0	341.0	17.1	64.0	54.1	407.7
1915	2,840.4	1,814.6	451.8	16.0	69.3	60.5	428.2
1916	2,981.4	1,755.5	580.4	17.7	72.7	77.1	478.0
1917	3,244.2	1,812.6	780.1	18.6	79.1	77.7	476.1
1918	3,063.6	1,775.6	662.8	17.6	57.4	95.4	454.5
1919	3,104.0	1,904.5	571.8	17.9	70.0	56.8	483.0
1920	2,883.6	1,821.3	411.9	15.9	75.2	75.9	483.4
1921	3,032.1	1,865.0	477.3	13.7	78.9	95.5	501.7
1922	3,396.8	2,043.8	605.0	18.1	93.8	110.5	525.6
1923	3,304.2	1,849.8	613.8	20.6	106.0	170.9	543.1
1924	3,877.4	2,288.0	684.3	22.5	118.3	194.8	569.5
1925	4,096.0	2,413.5	748.4	22.3	127.6	196.0	588.2
1926	4,020.1	2,336.2	731.1	23.1	136.9	195.9	596.9
1927	4,245.6	2,590.7	649.5	22.0	142.4	193.4	647.6
1928	4,428.4	2,557.4	798.6	24.3	149.1	198.2	700.8
1929	4,450.4	2,405.8	976.1	21.8	156.4	208.0	682.3
1930	4,766.0	2,747.9	924.0	23.1	166.6	233.7	670.7

TABLE 3 (Continued)

Year	Total	Food Crop	Special Crop	Fiber Crop	Vege-tables [a]	Fruits [b]	Livestock & Poultry
1931	4,873.4	2,812.6	866.3	20.7	176.6	250.2	747.0
1932	5,586.1	3,301.5	1,024.7	22.1	191.6	290.8	755.4
1933	5,031.0	3,089.8	721.1	23.2	197.5	289.8	709.6
1934	5,484.3	3,382.7	752.2	35.6	204.2	316.0	793.6
1935	5,884.6	3,403.3	1,058.6	46.9	213.7	306.6	855.5
1936	6,114.2	3,566.6	1,043.1	40.1	227.4	351.9	885.1
1937	6,199.5	3,497.3	1,156.0	46.3	216.4	365.9	917.6
1938	6,489.2	3,682.7	1,210.7	58.2	208.3	377.3	952.0
1939	6,553.7	3,375.5	1,673.3	85.2	195.1	367.4	857.2
1940	5,641.4	3,005.9	1,341.6	61.3	190.7	340.3	701.6
1941	5,563.8	3,186.2	1,183.2	63.1	179.6	355.5	596.2
1942	5,639.5	3,056.3	1,418.2	76.1	186.1	340.6	562.2
1943	5,385.9	2,889.7	1,345.0	51.7	168.3	258.8	672.4
1944	4,540.9	2,804.5	1,096.0	38.9	160.2	142.9	298.4
1945	2,721.8	1,726.5	509.0	17.2	148.7	91.0	229.4
1946	3,217.1	2,472.3	153.9	14.2	170.7	121.9	194.1
1947	3,767.1	2,778.2	217.7	28.5	248.0	253.9	240.8
1948	4,478.4	3,004.8	504.1	71.2	240.5	270.8	387.0
1949	5,221.7	3,356.7	937.4	52.2	262.2	238.0	357.2
1950	5,905.5	3,855.3	883.9	43.5	288.4	241.7	592.7
1951	6,085.6	3,936.1	727.5	60.8	299.7	249.1	812.4
1952	6,649.5	4,201.9	876.9	112.7	303.5	264.8	889.7
1953	7,480.0	4,393.3	1,296.4	47.1	305.9	251.2	1,186.1
1954	7,508.7	4,613.8	1,040.7	78.4	314.6	239.6	1,221.6
1955	7,480.8	4,459.0	1,037.3	112.0	328.6	264.9	1,279.0
1956	8,144.4	4,959.7	1,120.6	101.1	333.3	258.4	1,371.3
1957	8,867.2	5,242.7	1,260.3	120.7	356.5	306.9	1,580.1
1958	9,402.3	5,401.7	1,307.1	159.8	372.0	363.4	1,798.3
1959	9,331.2	5,322.6	1,367.3	182.8	375.0	366.9	1,716.6
1960	9,338.9	5,517.7	1,204.8	163.8	402.2	418.0	1,632.4

a. Total vegetable production for 1901–1917 is estimated to be 2.5 percent of gross value of agricultural production valued at 1952–1956 prices.

b. Total fruit production for 1901–1908 is estimated to be 2.7 percent of the gross value of agricultural production valued at 1952–1956 average farm prices.

Source: Physical production data of 1901 through 1943 taken from Taiwan, Department of Statistics, *Statistical Summary of Taiwan for the Past 51 Years*, Tables 203, 204, 205, 206, 207, and 208; data for 1944 and 1955 from Joint Commission on Rural Reconstruction, *Taiwan Agricultural Statistics: 1901–1955*, pp. 20–113; data for 1956–1960 from Taiwan, Department of Agriculture and Forestry, *Taiwan Agricultural Yearbook: 1961*, pp. 35–205. Farm product prices for 1952–1956 taken from *ibid*. Estimates of seeds and feeds based on Ralph N. Gleason, *Taiwan Food Balance: 1935–1954*.

of seventy-six different agricultural products. Although they used a different base period, that is, 1935–1937, their method basically is not different from the method used here. As they pointed out:

In order to eliminate the price changes over time on the compilation of aggregate value output as an indicator of agricultural inprovement and development over a period of time, a Laspeyres formula has been developed for computing aggregate value output in terms of constant prices in the selected base period.[7]

Despite this similarity, the two indices are different for the following two reasons: (1) The coverage of the two indices is slightly different since Hsieh and Lee selected seventy-six different products. Because the detailed list of the products covered in their index is not known, there is no way to determine how the difference in coverage has influenced the two indices. (2) More fundamentally, the output index they compiled is actually an index of gross agricultural production. This can be clearly seen from the following statement:

There are generally two kinds of concepts of agricultural products: gross product and net product. Their relation could be represented by the following equation: Net product = gross product − (depreciation of capital + expenses of intermediate goods).[8]

They believe that "gross product is more important than net product for meeting the demands in Taiwan." [9] Consequently, the gross product concept is the one they used to compile their output index. Presumably, seeds and feeds should be classified as intermediate product; they are not then excluded from gross product. If the ratio of seeds and feeds to total gross agricultural production changed over this period of time, the two indices, one based on gross output and another based on gross product (inclusive of seeds and feeds), will of course differ.

A comparison between the two indices is made and shown in Table 4 and Figure 2. As expected, the two indices are different but move very closely together.

7. S. C. Hsieh and T. H. Lee, *An Analytical Review of Agriculture in Taiwan: An Input-Output and Productivity Approach,* p. 19.
8. *Ibid.*
9. *Ibid.,* p. 20.

TABLE 4

Comparison of the Two Agricultural Output Indices,
1935–1956

(1935–1937 = 100)

Year	Hsieh & Lee's Index (1935–1937 prices)	Index Compiled in This Study (1952–1956 prices)
1935	97.53	97.01
1936	101.21	100.79
1937	101.27	102.20
1938	105.74	106.97
1939	106.50	108.04
1940	92.62	93.00
1941	92.30	91.72
1942	94.02	92.96
1943	90.30	88.79
1944	78.57	74.86
1945	48.35	44.87
1946	55.70	51.55
1947	68.27	62.10
1948	77.06	73.82
1949	90.97	86.08
1950	102.16	97.35
1951	104.73	100.32
1952	112.88	109.62
1953	126.25	123.30
1954	126.86	123.78
1955	124.79	123.32
1956	136.91	134.26

Source: Hsieh and Lee's index is taken from S. C. Hsieh and T. H. Lee, *An Analytical Review*, Appendix A, Table 1; our index is computed from Table 1.

Figure 2

COMPARISON OF HSIEH AND LEE'S OUTPUT INDEX
WITH INDEX COMPILED IN THIS STUDY

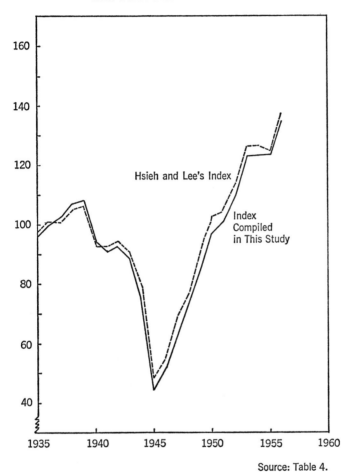

Source: Table 4.

Chapter 3

A REVIEW OF THE PAST GROWTH OF TAIWAN'S AGRICULTURAL OUTPUT

The main concern of this study is the growth in Taiwan's agricultural output and the means by which the increased output was achieved. Changes in output are consequences of changes in inputs broadly defined. This chapter reviews the past growth experience in Taiwan's agricultural output. Changes in input will be discussed in the following two chapters.

Changes in agricultural output between any two dates reflect both long-term, fundamental changes in agricultural supply function and short-term, irregular disturbances. The causes of changes and their interpretation are therefore different. The annual rates of change in agricultural output are presented in Table 5 and Figure 3. Rates of change for a number of selected pairs of years are shown in Table 6.

The annual rate of change of Taiwan's agricultural output was dominated by short-term fluctuation, as shown in Figure 3. The sharpest rise in agricultural output was recorded as high as 28.65 percent between 1902 and 1903; the greatest drop was as much as 40.06 percent between 1944 and 1945. Of the 59 annual changes, only 6 were changes of less than 1.0 percent point. Whereas 18 were changes between 1.0 to 5.0 percent, 35 were more than 5.0 percent. A possible explanation of this wide year-to-year fluctuation in agricultural output may be that agricultural production as a rule is vulnerable to natural conditions. This is especially noticeable in the case of Taiwan; because Taiwan is a small island, any change in natural conditions, favorable or unfavorable, is likely to affect the agricultural production of the whole island.

Aside from the extremely irregular short-term fluctuations, the period under review experienced a steady growth in agricultural output except for the interruption at the end of World War II when agricultural production and other economic organization of Taiwan nearly collapsed. The long-term growth rate of agricultural output for the whole period from 1901 to 1960 was 3.14 percent. Agricultural output grew

TABLE 5

Growth Rate of Gross Farm Output, 1901–1960

Year	Growth Rate	Year	Growth Rate
1901		1931	2.25
1902	1.08	1932	14.62
1903	28.65	1933	− 9.94
1904	11.94	1934	9.01
1905	5.68	1935	7.30
1906	− 3.75	1936	3.90
1907	8.63	1937	1.40
1908	5.11	1938	4.67
1909	1.89	1939	0.99
1910	− 2.41	1940	−14.92
1911	5.64	1941	− 1.38
1912	−10.02	1942	1.36
1913	13.75	1943	− 4.50
1914	− 4.25	1944	−15.69
1915	8.29	1945	−40.06
1916	4.96	1946	14.89
1917	8.81	1947	20.47
1918	− 6.58	1948	18.88
1919	1.33	1949	16.60
1920	− 7.10	1950	13.10
1921	5.15	1951	3.05
1922	12.03	1952	9.27
1923	− 2.73	1953	12.49
1924	17.35	1954	0.38
1925	5.64	1955	− 0.37
1926	− 1.85	1956	8.87
1927	5.61	1957	8.87
1928	4.30	1958	6.03
1929	0.50	1959	− 0.76
1930	7.09	1960	0.08

Source: Computed from Table 3.

at an annual average rate of 2.60 percent for the period 1901–1944. For the postwar years from 1945 to 1960, agricultural output grew at an average of 8.57 percent a year. As year-to-year changes are great in the case of Taiwan, the choice of period for comparison is significant. For example, the average annual growth rate for the prewar period ending at 1945 was 1.35 percent. If 1944 is taken as the last year of the prewar

TABLE 6

Growth Rate of Gross Farm Output, Selected Years

	1901	1905	1910	1915	1920	1925	1930	1935	1940	1945	1950	1955
1905	11.37	—	—	—	—	—	—	—	—	—	—	—
1910	5.94	1.79	—	—	—	—	—	—	—	—	—	—
1915	4.63	2.05	2.31	—	—	—	—	—	—	—	—	—
1920	3.47	1.46	1.30	0.30	—	—	—	—	—	—	—	—
1925	4.25	2.89	3.26	3.73	7.27	—	—	—	—	—	—	—
1930	4.05	2.92	3.21	3.51	5.15	3.08	—	—	—	—	—	—
1935	4.09	3.15	3.43	3.71	4.87	3.69	4.31	—	—	—	—	—
1940	3.44	2.57	2.70	2.78	3.41	2.16	1.70	−0.84	—	—	—	—
1945	1.35	0.40	0.20	−0.14	−0.23	−2.02	−3.66	−7.42	−13.56	—	—	—
1950	2.83	2.10	2.14	2.11	2.42	1.47	1.08	0.02	0.46	16.76	—	—
1955	3.01	2.37	2.44	2.45	2.76	2.03	1.82	1.21	1.90	10.64	4.64	—
1960	3.14	2.56	2.64	2.68	2.98	2.38	2.27	1.86	2.55	8.57	4.69	4.54

Source: Computed from Table 3.

Figure 3

YEAR-TO-YEAR FLUCTUATION OF AGRICULTURAL OUTPUT,
1901–1960

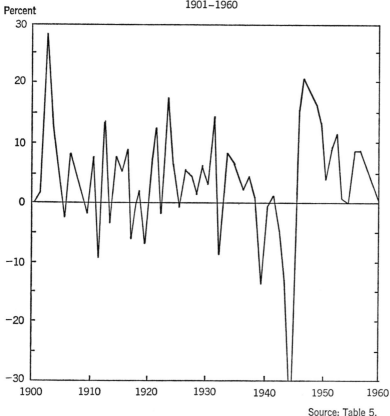

Source: Table 5.

period, growth rate for that period would become 2.60 percent, which is
almost twice as high as the average annual rate for 1901–1945. Similarly, the rate of growth for the postwar years would be 8.13 percent
instead of 8.57 percent if 1946 were taken as the beginning year for
the period. How then is the performance in the prewar years to be
appraised in comparison with that in the postwar period? As shown in
Table 6, the rates of growth for 1901–1905 and 1945–1950 were 11.37
and 16.76 percent, respectively, which by any reasonable standard can
be considered as very high and hardly normal. The historical back-
ground of the two periods warrants this judgment. Taiwan was ceded
to Japan in 1895 after China was defeated in the first Sino-Japanese

War. However, military resistance and violent movements for independence organized and led by local inhabitants against Japanese
occupation was not ended until 1902;[1] only then did social order
and economic organizations rapidly recover from disorders and chaos.
The high rate of growth in agricultural output of the period 1901–
1905 was therefore the temporary result of the recovery of the
setback. When Japan began preparing and later launched the war in the
Pacific, Taiwan's agricultural production was deflected from its long-
term growth pattern. Agriculture lost its priority, and projects to improve agricultural production were discontinued as all efforts were di-
rected to the war. Irrigation and drainage systems suffered from lack of
repair and maintenance and from Allied air raids. Moreover, the long-
established and close economic tie between industrial Japan proper and
her major agricultural supplier, Taiwan, was almost severed. As a
result, Taiwan was no longer able to import badly needed commercial
fertilizers from Japan. When Taiwan was restored to China in 1945,
agricultural production had declined so much that the total food output
was not enough to feed its population: in the prewar years, Taiwan had
set a record of exporting over 700,000 metric tons of brown rice, mainly
to Japan.[2] This one fact alone is sufficient to describe Taiwan's agricultural situation at the end of World War II. Therefore, the years from
1945 through 1950 were again a period of reconstruction and recovery
in Taiwan; accordingly, the rate of growth attained during that period
should not be considered as normal and representative.

If any comparison of growth rate between prewar and postwar periods is meaningful, the two periods of reconstruction and recovery should
be excluded from consideration. If wartime years were also disregarded, the growth rate for prewar period from 1906 to 1939 would be
3.32 percent; the postwar growth rate fell then to an average of 4.69
percent a year. Note that the year of 1939 was the peak year of
agricultural production in Taiwan before the war. Not until 1952 did
Taiwan break this previous record in its agricultural production. If
1952 is regarded as the year ending the postwar reconstruction period,
the growth rate for the postwar period then became 3.22 percent, which
is slightly lower than the prewar rate of 3.32 percent. A plot of the
gross agricultural output data for 1901–1960 on a semi-logarithm time

1. Yosaburo Takekoshi, *Japanese Rule in Formosa,* pp. 92–101.
2. Taiwan Provincial Food Bureau, *Taiwan Food Statistics Book,* p. 99.

series chart shows that 1953 growth in agricultural output began to swing back, after the great departure of 1942–1952, to the long-term linear trend (see Figure 4). By taking years on, or closer to, the linear trend as bases of comparison, the growth rate for 1905–1940 was 2.57 percent; it was 3.22 percent for the period 1953–1960. Because the year of 1939 was far off the linear trend, it seems to be more appropriate to take the long-term growth rate of 2.57 percent of 1905–1940, instead of the growth rate of 3.32 percent of 1906–1939, as the representative growth rate for the prewar period. The comparison of growth rates for the two periods cannot, admittedly, be conclusive because the choice of period for comparison affects the rates obtained. Nevertheless, from the evidences presented above, one can conclude that growth in agricultural output in the postwar period has been maintained at a rate at least as high as that of the prewar period even though less favorable conditions have prevailed in the postwar period.

Figure 4

INDEX OF AGRICULTURAL OUTPUT,
1901–1960

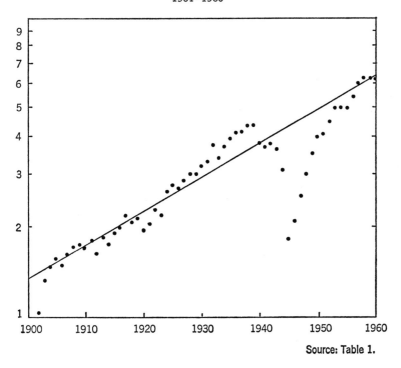

Source: Table 1.

The following table summarizes and lists rates of growth for all alternative choices of periods discussed here to compare the postwar growth in agricultural output with that of the prewar period.

Together with supply shifts for individual crops, changes in demand conditions for agricultural products, as a result of changes in income, taste, and other factors, will also have a bearing upon the composition of agricultural output.[3] Table 8 summarizes the changes in agricultural output composition during the period.

TABLE 7

Growth Rates of Prewar and Postwar Periods

Prewar Period	Compound Rate	Postwar Period	Compound Rate
1901–1945	1.35	1945–1960	8.57
1901–1944	2.60	1950–1960	4.67
1901–1940	3.44	1946–1960	8.13
1905–1940	2.57	1953–1960	3.22
1906–1945	0.05		
1906–1940	2.76		
1906–1939	3.32		

It is a generally accepted fact that although income elasticity for food products as a whole is less than unity, some individual products have higher income elasticities than others.[4] As income increases, the demand for products with high income elasticity will increase relative to that for cheap energy cereal foods. According to the U. S. data, considerably more citrus fruits and tomatoes were consumed per capita in 1949 than in 1909; in descending order, more dairy products, leafy green and yellow vegetables, sugar, eggs, coffee and tea, fats and oil, and dry beans were consumed in 1949 than in 1909.[5] The size of their increase during that time interval is not important. What is important, as inferred from these data, is that vegetables, fruits, livestock, and

3. T. W. Schultz considers that five factors will affect demand for agricultural products: income, taste, techniques applicable within consuming units, population, and other institutional and organizational arrangements. Schultz, *The Economic Organization of Agriculture,* p. 5.
4. Income elasticity for food products differs from one community to another. Schultz classifies communities into three types. Communities which use three-fourths or even more of their income for food are classified as type 1, whose income elasticity for food is in the neighborhood of unity. Schultz, *ibid.,* ch. 5.
5. *Ibid.,* Table 5–2.

poultry products have higher income elasticities than cereal foods. Changes in the composition of agricultural production, as shown in Table 8, are in part influenced by demand conditions, and those changes fit well into the normal pattern of change associated with the process of growth. The percentage share of food products in the total farm output declined about 17 percent from 71.03 percent in 1901–1905 to 58.66 percent in 1956–1960; the percentage share of vegetables climbed to 4.08 percent in 1956–1960 from 2.44 percent in 1901–1905—a 67-percent increase—and the percentage share of fruits increased 45 percent from 2.62 percent to 3.80 percent in the total during the same period. Livestock and poultry products also showed a 26-percent increase.

TABLE 8

Percent Output Composition of Agriculture,
1901–1960

Period	Food Crops	Special Crops	Fibre Crops	Vege-tables	Fruits	Livestock & Poultry	Total
1901–1905	71.03	8.91	0.81	2.44	2.62	14.19	100.00
1906–1910	67.74	11.99	0.76	2.44	2.65	14.42	100.00
1911–1915	65.14	14.18	0.59	2.44	2.18	15.17	100.00
1916–1920	59.37	19.68	0.57	2.32	2.51	15.55	100.00
1921–1925	59.08	17.67	0.55	2.96	4.33	15.41	100.00
1926–1930	57.68	18.62	0.52	3.43	4.70	15.05	100.00
1931–1935	59.53	16.47	0.55	3.66	5.41	14.38	100.00
1936–1940	55.26	20.72	0.94	3.35	5.82	13.91	100.00
1941–1945	57.28	23.27	1.04	3.53	4.99	9.89	100.00
1946–1950	68.74	11.99	0.93	5.38	5.01	7.95	100.00
1951–1955	61.37	14.14	1.17	4.41	3.61	15.30	100.00
1956–1960	58.66	13.89	1.61	4.08	3.80	17.96	100.00

As shown in Table 8, the composition of agricultural products does not change consistently in the expected direction throughout the period. Most notable is the sharp fall in the share of special crops, livestock, and poultry products and the equally sharp rise in the share of food crops. The change in the opposite direction from the long-term trend occurred during the period from 1946 to 1950 when the recovery of Taiwan's agriculture was taking place. In 1945 the substantial decline in income and output pushed the total farm output nearly back to the 1913 level. It is very probable that the adversity in income explains the change in output combination in 1945 and the following years as well.

Chapter 4

CHANGES IN TAIWAN'S AGRICULTURAL INPUT: LABOR

Increases in output can be either a result of changes in input or a result of changes in technology or both. Using T. W. Schultz's terms,[1] the part of the increment of output that is attributable to the increase in input is the "explained output"; while the residual part not so attributed is the "unexplained output," i.e., unexplained by conventional input changes. To follow the convention, changes in the explained output are considered a result of change in labor, land, working capital, and fixed capital. Agriculture in an underdeveloped economy is characterized by a high labor-to-capital ratio; labor so far is still the single most important input in agricultural production of such an economy. A meaningful analysis of change in agricultural productivity, either in terms of a single input or in terms of aggregate input, requires a reasonably accurate estimation of labor input and its change over time. This chapter is devoted to a discussion of the labor engaged in Taiwan's agricultural production during the period. Land input, fixed capital, and working capital input will be discussed in the following chapter.

Input is a flow concept. The measurement of labor input is, accordingly, the measurement of services rendered by agricultural workers during a given period of time. This necessarily calls for a clear definition of a working day in terms of a given length of time, a simple task in industrial production where a working day is clearly defined but not a feasible one in the case of agriculture. First, there is no such thing as a working day with the same length of time which is applicable to each individual worker in agriculture. Moreover, the length of a working day for an individual varies from one season to another, even from one day to another. The nature of agricultural production demands this flexibility. Although the difficulty of defining a working day in agriculture can be partially overcome in advanced countries by using data obtained

1. "Reflections on Agricultural Production, Output, and Supply," *Journal of Farm Economics,* XXXVIII (August 1956), 748–762.

from extensive empirical studies, underdeveloped countries still have no reliable studies of this kind.

In contrast to the measurement of input flow, the measurement of total gainfully occupied population in agriculture is that of a stock. The stock of gainfully occupied population in agriculture is taken here to be proportional to labor input since reliable data on labor input are not available.[2] Relative changes in the stock of gainfully occupied population in agriculture are taken to be the same as relative changes in agricultural labor input. This procedure requires information on the size of labor force in agriculture and rate of participation of labor force.

The size of the agricultural labor force is not an observed magnitude in Taiwan; consequently, it has to be derived from the available agricultural population figure. How one defines the term agricultural population will then definitely affect the size of agricultural labor force and therefore the size of gainfully occupied population in agriculture. There are two different sets of data on Taiwan's agricultural population: one from the census enumerations of Taiwan and the other from household registration records. Seven censuses were taken in Taiwan during the period of Japanese occupation. The first census was taken in 1905, the second in 1915, and so on for every five years thereafter. Although the first two censuses were called household surveys to avoid possible suspicion on the part of inhabitants of the island, they were in essence a modern census.[3] The most recent census taken was in 1956, which was seventeen years after the preceding one. However, only the first three censuses provided data on agricultural population.

2. According to a sample census report on Taiwan's agriculture, which was taken in 1956, the average working day for agricultural operators and main workers was 298 man-days per farm household; each farm household had 1.56 operator and main worker. Thus, the average working day per farm worker was about 200 man-days. Taiwan, Committee of Sample Census of Agriculture, *Report on the 1956 Sample Census of Agriculture,* pp. 102–109. According to another study, the average working day per rice cultivator was 162 man-days for 1936–1937. Research Institute, Bank of Taiwan, *Agricultural Economy of Taiwan,* p. 38. Hsieh and Lee developed a labor input series in terms of labor required by crops and livestock for the period 1935–1956. Since the basis of their estimation was not known to the writer, their series is not used here. The average working day is affected by two factors: the size of the average farm and the degree of land utilization. Whereas the size of the average farm declined during the period, the degree of land utilization has greatly increased. The average working day per worker has probably moved upward.

3. Taiwan, Bureau of Accounting and Statistics, *The Results of the Seventh Population Census of Taiwan: 1940.*

The household registration records furnished, among other things, unbroken annual statistics on Taiwan's agricultural population from 1901 to 1960.[4] It forms the basis of estimating the annual stock of gainfully occupied population in agriculture. However, the agricultural population recorded here is considerably different from the census data; agricultural population from the household registration record is consistently smaller than the census enumerations of agricultural population (see Table 9). The differences cannot be reconciled even with the two adjusted to the same date.[5] Presumably, the discrepancy is the consequence of different definitions of agricultural population used in the two enumerations. Agricultural population in the household registration record is classified into three subgroups—owner-cultivators, part-owners, and tenants. This classification explains why the two enumerations differ: farm hired laborers were not included in the agricultural population statistics in the household registration record. Conceptually and statistically, farm hired labor is indeed a very difficult problem to handle; yet, one cannot solve the problem by excluding hired labor completely from agricultural population. Thus, if the data on agricultural population from the household registration record are going to be used as a basis to estimate labor input, a certain adjustment has to be made for hired labor.

Assuming that the difference between the household registration enumeration of agricultural population and the census enumeration, after being adjusted to be a year-end statistic, represents the size of the farm hired labor, the ratio of farm hired labor to total population can then be established for the three census years, i.e., 1905, 1915, and 1920. These ratios are 4.27 percent, 3.34 percent, and 4.67 percent, respectively. Official data on farm hired labor are available for the period from 1947 to 1960; the same ratio therefore can also be calculated for 1947, which is found to be 3.40 percent. The ratio of farm hired labor to total population for all inter-census years between 1901 and 1947 can be interpolated and extrapolated by assuming a constant rate of change. The population of farm hired labor of each individual year is obtained

4. Data of agricultural population can be found in *Agricultural Statistics, Statistical Summary,* and Taiwan, Department of Agriculture and Forestry, *Taiwan Agricultural Yearbook.*
5. Agricultural population from the household registration record was a year-end statistic, whereas the census was taken on October 1 each census year.

by multiplying the ratio of farm hired labor population by the corresponding total population figure. The adjusted agricultural population is the original agricultural population series from the household registration record plus the farm hired labor population so estimated; the adjusted population in agriculture provides the basis of estimating the labor input. The procedure of estimating and adjusting agricultural population of Taiwan is necessary and essential to gauge the labor input

TABLE 9

Agricultural Population, Selected Years

Year	Household Registration Data	Census Data [b]
1905	1,961,556	2,038,795
1915	2,252,850 [a]	2,312,312
1920	2,261,856 [a]	2,370,723
1925	2,339,647	—

a. The figure for 1915 is the average of 1914 and 1916; the 1920 figure is the average of 1919 and 1921.
b. Not including forestry.
Source: Household registration data from *Agricultural Statistics*, p. 7; and *Statistical Summary*, Table 194. Census data from *Statistical Summary*, Table 59.

because agricultural employment data is limited to six census years.[6] A complete agricultural employment series for the whole period has to be estimated based on the agricultural population series so obtained.

The rate of participation of the agricultural labor force is calculated for the six census years, 1905, 1915, 1920, 1930, 1940, and 1956 based on the census's agricultural employment data. To define labor force in the conventional Western sense, i.e., population over 14 years of age and under 65, is not appropriate in Taiwan. The rate of participation so obtained is persistently over 100 percent.[7] The agricultural labor force

6. Census of 1925 and 1935 provided no information on agricultural employment.
7. This refers only to male labor force. For example, the size of labor force, defined in the above manner, in 1905 was 710,493; 757,431 were gainfully occupied, according to the census enumeration.

defined in the Western conventional manner understates the actual size of labor force. It is not uncommon in rural Taiwan, as well as in other underdeveloped countries, for children under 14 and adults over 65 to be actively engaged in agricultural production. Therefore, the portion of agricultural population with age over 12 is defined here as agricultural labor force. Admittedly, this definition tends to overestimate by including people over 65 in the labor force, but, in the meantime, it excludes those child laborers under the age of 12, which makes the size of the labor force estimated here smaller than the actual size of the labor force in agriculture. The agricultural labor force so defined and the series so obtained can be regarded as reasonably satisfactory. Table 11 shows the ratios of gainfully occupied population to working age population in Japan estimated by Professor S. Hijikata. Although the two series are not directly comparable, the ratio of gainfully occupied to working age

TABLE 10

Rate of Participation of Labor Force in
Agriculture, Selected Years

Year	Gainfully Occupied [a]		Labor Force [b] (Over 12)		Rate of Participation [c]	
	Male	Female	Male	Female	Male	Female
1905	728,431	341,660	770,680	696,982	94.50%	49.00%
1915	773,449	420,929	832,481	770,704	92.90%	54.60%
1920	757,043	375,226	846,383	809,227	89.40%	46.40%
1930	851,245	328,115	918,402	867,672	92.70%	37.80%
1940	910,753	477,479	1,022,122	995,252	89.10%	47.98%
1956	1,094,302	303,563	1,547,281	1,493,133	70.73%	20.30%

a. Gainfully occupied population in forestry is not included.

b. Labor force in agriculture is the portion of the agricultural population over 12. Census agricultural population data are used for 1905, 1915, and 1920. For 1930, 1940, and 1956 agricultural population has been adjusted to census date, and farm hired laborers are included.

c. Rate of participation is the ratio of gainfully occupied population to total labor force in agriculture.

Source: Data of gainfully occupied population and total agricultural population for 1905, 1915, 1920 and 1930 are taken from *Statistical Summary*, Table 59; data of 1940 from Taiwan, Committee of Sample Census of Agriculture, *A Report on the 1956 Sample Census of Agriculture*, Table 11. For the source of age distribution of the population, see Table 15.

population in agriculture obtained here seems to be more reasonable and acceptable (see Table 10).[8]

Women laborers also occupy a large share in the total agricultural labor force and contribute importantly to agricultural production; they should not be excluded from the category of agricultural labor force. Separate estimates are made for women laborers in agriculture because women's employment statistics are less satisfactory.

TABLE 11

Rate of Occupied Population to Working Age Population, Selected Years, Japan

Year	Ratio
1880	90.6
1885	95.9
1890	98.2
1900	95.7
1905	93.8
1910	92.3
1915	88.7
1920	88.1
1925	85.6
1930	82.1
1935	81.4
1940	79.2

Source: Quoted from Kazushi Ohkawa and others, *The Growth Rate of the Japanese Economy Since 1878*, p. 148.

The rate of participation of male as well as female labor force in agriculture for all inter-census years can therefore be interpolated and extrapolated based on the rate of participation of labor force in each census year. In using the rate of participation in census years to estimate the employment in agriculture for the whole period, two assumptions are made: (1) the rate of participation from the census enumerations on each census date is representative of the average and normal rate of participation through the census year, and (2) the rate of

8. Professor Hijikata's estimates before 1900 are somewhat erratic.

change in agricultural employment between census years is constant. The results are presented in Table 12. Whether the employment series so derived is proportional to labor input in agriculture depends inevitably on the composition of the gainfully occupied population defined in the census enumerations. It is conceivable that a fully occupied main farm operator and a part-time hired farm hand can both be classified as gainfully occupied. The census enumeration used here presumably made no such distinction. Nevertheless, farm hired labor accounted only for a small share in the total agricultural employment, and its share remained extremely stable in the range from 3.3 to 4.3 percent of the total agricultural employment.[9] Indiscriminate treatment of the individual components of the gainfully occupied population does no harm so long as the composition is stable over time.

Gainfully occupied population was steadily increasing except during the years between 1916 and 1923. Between the years of 1915 to 1920, Taiwan was struck by three near-epidemic diseases.[10] This was the principal reason for the decline in agricultural employment of the period as well as in the succeeding years. Throughout the whole period, the rate of growth in agricultural employment is much slower than the rate of growth in total population, as shown in Table 13. This result, however, should not be interpreted as a result of the economic transformation in terms of relative growth between agricultural and nonagricultural sectors. As is clearly shown in Table 14, the occupational structure of Taiwan from 1901 to 1940 was virtually unchanged in terms of percentage employed in agricultural and nonagricultural sectors. Japanese colonial policy toward Taiwan deliberately placed its emphasis on the island's agriculture with the intention of developing Taiwan as Japan's major supplier of food products. Nonagricultural jobs, generated from the establishment of modern transportation, sugar-refining industry, and other light industries, were strictly reserved for the Japanese nationals.

The slow growth of agricultural employment is caused by the following two factors: First, during the period 1901–1960, Taiwan witnessed a rapid increase in its population. A high rate of population growth is

9. Farm hired labor and their families accounted for 3.3 to 4.3 percent of the total population. Proportionally, they also accounted for 3.3 to 4.3 percent of the total agricultural employment.

10. George W. Barclay, *Colonial Development and Population in Taiwan,* p. 12.

TABLE 12

Gainfully Occupied Population in Agriculture,
1901–1960

Year	Gainfully Occupied [a]		Gainfully Occupied [b]	Index
	Male	Female	Man-Equivalent	
1901	730	320	922	100.00
1902	736	327	932	101.08
1903	739	332	938	101.74
1904	745	339	949	102.93
1905	755	348	963	104.45
1906	757	352	969	105.10
1907	771	363	989	107.27
1908	770	369	991	107.48
1909	740	359	955	103.58
1910	773	381	1,001	108.57
1911	775	390	1,010	109.54
1912	788	400	1,028	111.50
1913	795	410	1,041	112.91
1914	799	418	1,050	113.88
1915	800	428	1,056	114.53
1916	805	424	1,059	114.86
1917	804	415	1,053	114.21
1918	803	406	1,046	113.45
1919	803	396	1,041	112.91
1920	791	379	1,016	110.20
1921	783	368	1,004	108.89
1922	784	361	1,000	108.46
1923	800	362	1,018	110.41
1924	817	362	1,034	112.15
1925	832	361	1,048	113.67
1926	836	355	1,049	113.77
1927	836	347	1,044	113.23
1928	846	343	1,052	114.10
1929	837	335	1,038	112.58
1930	855	329	1,053	114.21
1931	863	343	1,069	115.94
1932	854	351	1,064	115.40
1933	866	367	1,086	117.79
1934	878	383	1,108	120.17
1935	897	404	1,139	123.54
1936	909	422	1,162	126.03
1937	909	435	1,170	126.90
1938	906	447	1,174	127.33
1939	906	461	1,183	128.31
1940	915	480	1,203	130.48

TABLE 12 (Continued)

Year	Gainfully Occupied [a] Male	Female	Gainfully Occupied [b] Man-Equivalent	Index
1941	928	475	1,213	131.56
1942	947	473	1,232	133.62
1943	958	466	1,238	134.27
1944	950	453	1,222	132.54
1945	945	441	1,209	131.13
1946	964	440	1,228	133.19
1947	969	425	1,225	132.86
1948	1,011	426	1,268	137.53
1949	1,030	411	1,277	138.50
1950	1,044	399	1,284	139.26
1951	1,069	391	1,304	141.43
1952	1,078	375	1,303	141.32
1953	1,089	358	1,304	141.43
1954	1,094	340	1,334	144.68
1955	1,100	323	1,295	140.46
1956	1,100	305	1,283	139.15
1957	1,100	310	1,285	139.37
1958	1,101	316	1,290	139.91
1959	1,104	320	1,297	140.67
1960	1,168	344	1,375	149.13

a. The method of estimation is as follows: (1) Gainfully occupied population in agriculture is obtained by multiplying the total labor force in agriculture by the rate of participation of each year. (2) Total labor force in agriculture is the portion of agricultural population over 12. As shown in Table 15, the age distribution of the total population is computed for 1905, 1915, 1920, 1925, 1930, 1935, 1940, and 1956. If the rate of change in age distribution of the total population is assumed constant, the age distribution of the total population for all years can be interpolated and extrapolated based on the ratios shown in Table 15. Age distribution of agricultural population is assumed to be the same as the age distribution of the whole population. (3) Labor force in agriculture is obtained by multiplying the agricultural population by the ratio of the population over 12 to the total population. (4) For agricultural population, see Appendix B. (5) Rate of participation is computed for 1905, 1915, 1920, 1930, 1940, and 1956. Again, assuming that the rate of change in the labor participation rate between any pair of years is constant, rate of participation for all other years can be established by interpolation and extrapolation based on the six rates of participation as shown in Table 10.

b. Female laborer is converted into male equivalent by using the ratio of 1 female labor equal to 0.6 male labor.

Source: See Tables 9, 10, 15, and Appendix B.

TABLE 13

*Rates of Population and Agricultural
Employment Growth*

(compound rate)

Period	Rate of Population Growth	Rate of Agricultural Employment Growth
1901–1910 [a]	1.1	0.85
1911–1920	1.1	0.05
1921–1930	2.0	0.25
1931–1940	2.4	1.18
1941–1950 [b]	1.9	0.32
1951–1960	3.2	0.55
1901–1944	1.7	0.60
1946–1960	4.1	0.80
1901–1960	2.2	0.70

a. Population of 1901 is interpolated from 1900 and 1902, which is recorded in Takakoshi's *Japanese Rule in Formosa*, p. 197.

b. Population of 1944 and 1946 was estimated from the data in Taiwan, Bureau of Accounting and Statistics, *Results of the Seventh Census of Taiwan: 1940*, Appendix 1, Table 1, by assuming that all Japanese left the island in these two years.

Source: Rate of population growth computed from data taken from: *Statistical Summary*, Table 49, for the period 1905–1943; data of 1949–1960 from Taiwan, Economic Research Center, *Taiwan Statistical Book*, p. 4; data of 1946–1948 from *Agricultural Statistics*, p. 7. For data of employment in agriculture, see Appendix B.

usually accompanied by a larger portion of population under age 12 (see Table 15). Consequently, the ratio of working age population to total population is bound to decline. Second, the slow rate of growth in agricultural employment is partially the result of declining rate of labor participation in agriculture (see Table 10). Most noticeable is the sharp change in the participation rate for female labor between 1940 and 1956. Given the definition of working-age population as used here, a decreasing trend in the rate of participation of labor force in agriculture can be regarded as a normal phenomenon in association with

TABLE 14

Occupation Structure, Selected Years
(percentage)

Year	Agriculture	Nonagriculture
1905	71.29	28.71
1915	71.50	28.50
1920	69.46	30.54
1930	66.87	33.13
1940	64.60[a]	35.40

a. Including forestry.
Source: 1905, 1915, 1920, and 1930 computed from data in *Statistical Summary*, Table 59; 1940 from Barclay, *Colonial Development*, p. 71.

economic development because people tend to prolong their educational and training period before they enter and engage in direct productive activities as income and educational opportunities increase. Therefore, the continuous decrease of the participation rate of labor force in agriculture is indicative of the fact that the working age needs an upward revision as development proceeds.[11] Other factors may be responsible in the case of sharp decline in the female participation rate in agriculture. The relatively high participation rate of 47.98 percent in 1940 probably was the result of war mobilization. This would have caused the changes in the female employment in the succeeding period to be misleadingly low.

The heavy influx of people, beginning in 1948, from China's mainland could be a factor in inflating the size of agricultural population. The total agricultural population increased by 50 percent between 1940 and 1956 (see Table 10), and, in turn, the size of the agricultural labor force increased. The labor participation rate in agriculture would have certainly been deflated if those immigrants who took up rural residence were classified as agricultural population but did not work on farms. Nevertheless, classifying the immigrants in this way could not have been a decisive factor for the decline in the participation rate of agricultural labor. According to the adjusted agricultural population as compiled

11. An increase in job opportunity off the farm could also cause a fall in the rate of participation of labor force in agriculture.

TABLE 15

Age Distribution of Population [a]

(percentage)

Census Year	0–11		12–14		15–60		Over 60	
	Male	*Female*	*Male*	*Female*	*Male*	*Female*	*Male*	*Female*
1905	27.98	28.05	6.19	5.74	62.88	60.54	2.95	5.66
1915	30.30	31.06	6.49	6.19	60.17	57.13	3.04	5.62
1920	29.86	30.48	7.06	6.92	60.01	57.00	3.07	5.60
1925	29.52	30.07	7.29	7.16	60.12	57.37	3.07	5.40
1930	34.02	34.54	6.25	6.19	56.95	54.48	2.78	4.79
1935	35.56	35.84	6.49	6.52	54.85	52.64	3.10	5.00
1940	37.03	36.54	6.89	6.80	52.64	51.46	3.44	5.20
1956	38.19	37.56	6.39	6.20	52.40	51.93	3.02	4.31

a. For all ethnic groups.
Source: Computed from data taken from *Statistical Summary*, *Results of the Seventh Census*, and *Report on the 1956 Sample Census*.

here, growth in agricultural population for 1946–1956 was at a 2.6-percent annual rate, which is very much in line with the rate of natural increase of 2.4 percent in the growth of population of Taiwan during the period from 1926–1943.[12]

12. According to George Barclay, the rates of natural increase were 23.9 and 24.4 per thousand for 1926–1935 and 1936–1943, respectively. Barclay, *A Report on Taiwan's Population*, p. 44.

Chapter 5

CHANGES IN TAIWAN'S AGRICULTURAL INPUTS: LAND, FIXED CAPITAL, AND WORKING CAPITAL

Land

Land, one of the major inputs of agricultural production, refers not only to the physical surface of the earth but to all the natural conditions pertaining to it, which include fertility, rainfall, soil moisture, and topographical conditions of the land. Although these natural conditions determine the quality of the land and consequently the contribution of the land as an input of agiculture to the total output, they cannot be quantified in any meaningful way. What is to be measured as land input here is only the surface of the land.

The total land area of Taiwan is measured as 3,596,121 hectares. More than two-thirds of the land area is mountainous and untillable; a mere one-fourth of the total is arable under present technical conditions.[1] The expansion of cultivated land area had virtually reached its limit in the late 1930s. During the first four decades of the century, the cultivated land area had been doubled from 376,000 hectares in 1901 to 860,000 hectares in 1940. The total cultivated area was still in the neighborhood of 860,000 hectares in 1960. It is apparent that the expansion in land area has become virtually impossible and ceased to be a contributing factor of the growth in Taiwan's agricultural output since 1940. This does not mean, however, that land is no longer a contributing factor to the increased output since 1940. As the horizontal expansion of land area became infeasible, an ever-growing agricultural output was made possible through the vertical expansion of land, that is, through the improvement in the quality of land and the increase in the degree of land utilization. Vertical expansion is clearly shown in the sharp rise in the crop area and paddy fields in the cultivated land total.

Improvement in the quality of land can take various forms, such as flood control, soil conservation, and the application of fertilizers. But the changes in irrigated land area and the increase in the paddy fields are

1. Taiwan, Bureau of Accounting and Statistics, *Taiwan Statistical Abstract,* No. 15, p. 1.

two observable phenomena taken here as the indicators of land improvement. During the period, the irrigated land area increased about 100 percent, the paddy fields increased about 160 percent, and the share of paddy fields increased 20 percent in the total of the cultivated land (see Table 16).[2] The conversion of dry land into the paddy field was

TABLE 16

Land Improvement, Selected Years

Year	Paddy Land to Cultivated Total, percent	Irrigated Land to Cultivated Total, percent
1905	48.8	31.1
1910	49.3	33.6
1915	49.0	34.6
1920	49.0	40.7
1925	48.2	45.2
1930	48.2	54.3
1935	57.6	56.1
1940	61.6	61.6
1945 [a]	61.8	60.3
1950	60.9	58.4
1955	61.0	54.7
1960	60.8	65.7

a. Estimated.

Source: Computed from data in *Statistical Summary*, Table 214 for 1901 through 1940. Data of 1950 taken from Taiwan, Bureau of Accounting and Statistics, *Taiwan Statistical Abstract*, No. 15, Table 50; data of 1955 and 1960 from *Agricultural Yearbook*, 1961 edition, p. 21.

especially active during the period from 1930 to 1940, and the irrigated land area increased mostly after 1920. The timing of the development cannot be merely regarded as a coincidence. Rather, the simultaneous development illustrates that a significant change in land use had occurred at the time when land utilization through acreage expansion was approaching its limits.

Unlike measurements of land improvement, changes in the crop area indicate clearly the improvement in the degree of land utilization. The measurement of crop area includes both the frequency of land utilization and changes in acreage; that is, if two crops are grown on the same acre

2. The increase is 60.8 percent divided by 48.8 percent.

of land, one following the other, the same piece of land is counted as two acres of crop area. The increase in crop area is the combined result of land expansion and the intensity of land utilization. If the increase in crop area is greater than the increase in land expansion, as is apparent in the case of Taiwan, the degree of intensity of land use has increased. In terms of a multiple-cropping index as the ratio of crop area to physical land area, the rate of intensity of land utilization has increased from 109.8 percent in 1905 to 179.2 percent in 1960—an increase of 65 percent (see Table 17). This is to say that the frequency of land use

TABLE 17

Land Utilization, Selected Years

Year	Crop Area[a] (hectare)	Index of Crop Area 1901 = 100	Multiple- Cropping Index
1905	685,987	135.7	109.8
1910	731,431	144.7	108.5
1915	812,266	160.7	116.0
1920	829,797	164.2	110.7
1925	925,009	183.0	119.3
1930	976,396	193.2	120.2
1935	1,090,174	215.6	131.2
1940	1,117,371	221.0	129.9
1945	867,819	171.7	106.4
1950	1,441,956	285.2	165.6
1955	1,466,909	292.0	168.0
1960	1,557,227	308.0	179.2

a. The crop area shown here is the sum of un-weighted planted areas of the 74 crops that are used in compiling the output index. The crop area as defined here measures the frequency of land utilization in a given year. For this reason, area planted to sugar cane has been converted to an annual basis by multiplying the actual area planted to sugar cane by 0.6667 because the average growing period for sugar cane is 18 months.

Source: Computed from data drawn from *Statistical Summary*, Tables 203, 204, 205, 206, 207, and 208 for the period 1901–1940; data for period 1941–1955 taken from *Agricultural Statistics*, Table 5A; for years between 1956 and 1960, from *Agricultural Yearbook*, 1961 edition.

has increased from about one crop per year to about two crops per year per unit of land. However, as one of the conventional input components in agriculture, land is measured here by the physical land area instead of crop area, because to take crop area as land input is really to disregard the contribution of technical progress to the increased output flow. Land input of the whole period is shown in Table 18.

TABLE 18

Land Input, 1901–1960

Unit: Hectare

Year	Total	Paddy Field	Dry Land	Index
1901	375,909	206,753	169,156	100.00
1902	437,465	245,388	192,077	116.38
1903	534,157	278,190	255,967	142.10
1904	625,299	303,196	322,103	166.34
1905	624,501	304,908	319,593	166.13
1906	633,647	309,615	324,032	168.56
1907	654,233	318,658	335,575	174.04
1908	650,233	322,800	327,438	172.98
1909	661,949	327,620	334,329	176.09
1910	674,100	332,372	341,728	179.32
1911	687,187	334,928	352,259	182.81
1912	689,889	335,955	353,931	183.52
1913	691,032	337,610	353,422	183.83
1914	693,173	339,593	353,580	184.40
1915	700,080	343,087	356,993	186.24
1916	716,205	347,879	368,326	190.53
1917	720,637	320,528	400,109	191.70
1918	732,255	341,479	390,776	194.80
1919	737,923	345,101	392,822	196.30
1920	749,419	367,177	382,242	199.36
1921	752,805	364,148	388,657	200.26
1922	750,540	365,002	385,538	199.66
1923	752,076	365,434	386,642	200.07
1924	761,800	368,642	391,158	202.66
1925	775,488	373,629	401,839	206.29
1926	790,044	382,093	407,951	210.17
1927	797,151	387,144	410,007	212.06
1928	806,754	391,714	415,040	214.61
1929	805,043	393,817	411,226	214.16
1930	812,116	396,670	415,446	216.04

TABLE 18 (Continued)

Year	Total	Paddy Field	Dry Land	Index
1931	810,277	398,709	411,568	215.55
1932	814,471	426,246	388,225	216.67
1933	820,047	436,934	383,113	218.15
1934	825,726	443,990	376,736	219.66
1935	831,003	478,689	352,314	221.06
1936	846,021	517,771	328,250	225.06
1937	856,689	528,061	328,628	227.10
1938	857,789	526,818	330,970	228.19
1939	859,550	530,100	329,450	228.66
1940	860,439	529,610	330,829	228.90
1941	859,446	527,981	331,465	228.63
1942	854,462	524,533	329,929	227.30
1943	846,986	519,861	327,125	225.32
1944	808,165	501,414	306,751	214.99
1945	816,017	504,709	311,308	217.08
1946	831,951	507,636	324,315	221.32
1947	833,952	516,378	317,574	221.85
1948	863,157	526,384	336,773	229.62
1949	864,864	528,097	336,767	230.07
1950	870,633	530,236	340,397	231.61
1951	873,871	533,804	340,067	232.47
1952	876,100	533,643	342,457	233.06
1953	872,738	533,316	339,422	232.17
1954	874,097	532,565	341,532	232.53
1955	873,002	532,688	340,314	232.04
1956	875,791	533,113	342,618	232.98
1957	873,263	533,144	340,118	232.31
1958	883,466	533,674	349,792	235.02
1959	877,740	528,762	348,978	233.50
1960	869,223	528,580	343,643	231.23

Source: Data of land area for 1901 through 1955 are taken from *Agricultural Statistics*, p. 11; data of 1956 to 1960 *Agricultural Yearbook*, 1960 edition.

Fixed Capital

Farm fixed capital includes farm service buildings, farm implements and equipment, and draft animals. Official data on farm houses, implements and equipment are so scattered and incomplete that they cannot be organized in any useful way.[3] In reviewing agricultural development in Japan for the period from 1878 to 1942, Toshio Shishido, for want of a better alternative, took the total volume of energy in agriculture as representing the fixed capital input.[4] For the same reason, the total animal horsepower in agriculture is to be regarded here as representing the fixed capital input with the implicit assumption that changes in animal energy in agriculture is proportional to the changes in total fixed capital in agriculture. However, the coverage of the capital series as constructed here is much narrower than Mr. Shishido's. While his series covered the total number of horses, cattles, motors, engines, and other sources of energy, the series here covers only animal energy in agriculture. The fixed capital input for Taiwan is presented in Table 19.

The fixed capital input of agriculture during the long period has a peculiar trend. It increased rapidly during the first decade of the period, but from 1912 to 1946 the fixed capital continuously declined. Although after the war the fixed capital increased steadily, the horsepower available in 1960 was just about the same as in 1908. The reason for the sluggishness of farm fixed capital is not quite clear. However, a breakdown of the fixed capital components sheds some light on the problem. Water buffalo and draft cattle are by far the two most important types of draft animals in Taiwan.[5] They serve entirely different purposes: water buffaloes are mainly employed for plowing and preparing fields; draft cattle are bred for pulling carts. While the number of water buffaloes remained relatively stable between the years 1910 to 1944, the population of draft cattle fell considerably. The decrease in draft cattle is obviously the main reason for the fall in fixed capital total (see Table

3. Professor Mo-Huan Hsing made an independent estimate of the values of farm houses and implements for 1950–1958. His estimates were based on the assumption that the average value of farm houses and implements per hectare could be regarded as constant under the existing farm techniques. He first obtained the value of farm houses and implements for 1953. By using the known capital formation figures of that period, he derived his series of the value of farm houses and implements for 1950 to 1958. His method cannot be used here since it requires data on capital formation which is not available. Hsing, *et al., Relationships between Agricultural and Industrial Development in Taiwan during 1950–1959*, p. 31.
4. "Japanese Agriculture: Productivity Trend and Development of Technique," *Journal of Farm Economics*, XLIII, No. 2 (May 1961), 285–295.
5. Draft animals referred to here include water buffaloes, draft cattle, Indian cattle, Western cattle, hybrid cattle, and horses.

TABLE 19

Fixed Capital Input, 1901–1960

Unit: 1,000 HP

Year	Horsepower [a]	Index	Year	Horsepower [a]	Index
1901	117.5	100.00	1931	191.7	163.15
1902	128.0	108.94	1932	183.7	156.34
1903	143.0	121.70	1933	193.2	164.42
1904	162.5	138.30	1934	197.7	168.26
1905	171.1	145.62	1935	195.3	166.21
1906	176.7	150.38	1936	185.9	158.21
1907	187.1	159.23	1937	179.4	152.68
1908	207.6	176.68	1938	162.9	138.64
1909	230.1	195.83	1939	162.9	138.64
1910	240.1	204.34	1940	150.4	128.00
1911	239.1	203.49	1941	154.9	131.83
1912	223.1	189.87	1942	156.4	133.11
1913	209.6	178.38	1943	162.9	138.64
1914	202.1	172.00	1944	166.9	142.04
1915	199.6	169.87	1945	146.2	124.42
1916	193.1	164.34	1946	140.5	119.57
1917	188.6	160.51	1947	149.3	127.06
1918	192.6	163.91	1948	155.3	132.17
1919	202.1	172.00	1949	178.8	152.17
1920	214.6	182.64	1950	182.7	155.49
1921	211.1	179.66	1951	187.7	159.74
1922	204.6	174.13	1952	191.7	163.15
1923	195.6	166.47	1953	195.2	166.13
1924	191.6	163.06	1954	203.3	173.02
1925	189.6	161.36	1955	206.2	175.49
1926	190.6	162.21	1956	207.2	176.34
1927	193.1	164.34	1957	207.2	176.34
1928	194.2	165.28	1958	209.7	178.47
1929	195.2	166.13	1959	210.1	178.81
1930	195.7	166.55	1960	210.1	178.81

a. The horsepower series contains only animal energy available in agriculture. To aggregate animal energy in agriculture the following coefficients are used: A normal horse is 0.6 horsepower, cattle are 0.5 horsepower. These coefficients are the same coefficients used for Japan by Toshio Shishido, "Japanese Agriculture," p. 294.

Source: Computed from data drawn from *Agricultural Statistics*, p. 109; and from *Agricultural Yearbook*, 1962 edition.

20). It is very probable that the decline in the draft cattle population
was one of the consequences of the development of modern transportation facilities during that period; the cattle cart became obsolete. This
possible explanation is supported by the fact that the number of draft
cattle born declined from 19,000 per year for 1910–1914 to 4,000 per
year for 1940–1944.[6] The cattle population increase in the postwar years
was largely attributable to the increase in the population of water
buffalo. The population of water buffalo has been relatively stationary

TABLE 20

Changes of the Cattle Population,
1910–1944

Period	Number of Water Buffalo	Number of Draft Cattle
1910–1914	291,278	152,100
1915–1919	276,453	111,961
1920–1924	300,000	103,661
1925–1929	292,225	86,999
1930–1934	298,014	76,963
1935–1939	281,212	60,374
1940–1944	263,630	40,740

Source: Computed from the data from *Statistical Summary*
Table 241, pp. 686–687.

during the period from 1901 to 1960, but it increased slightly in the
postwar period.[7] Very small farms cannot afford to support a draft
animal. Increased intensity of land utilization, on the other hand,
undoubtedly called for more animal energy in agriculture because the
population of water buffalo took an upward turn in the period from
1951 to 1960.

Admittedly, the fixed capital series as estimated here leaves much to
be desired. The peculiar trend of the series seems to be improbable; the
coverage of the series is undoubtedly narrow. However, the series

6. Computed from data drawn from *Statistical Summary*, Table 242, pp. 694–
695.
7. From 1878 to 1912 the total horsepower in Japan's agriculture showed a
similar trend to that in Taiwan; from 1,036,000 in 1878–1882, total horsepower
declined to 988,000 in 1888–1892 and then slowly increased to 1,168,000 in 1908–
1912. Shishido, "Japanese Agriculture."

should be regarded merely as a poor substitute used to overcome the problem of missing data on the true fixed capital input. Although the fixed capital series, as it stands, suffers from this serious defect, the consequence of missing data on the aggregate input (hence, to the computed residuals) is small and tolerable because fixed capital accounted for only 10.85 percent in the aggregate.[8]

Working Capital

Working capital input is represented here by the series of commercial fertilizers consumed. It is implicitly assumed that other current inputs vary in proportion with commercial fertilizers (see Table 21). The

TABLE 21

Working Capital Input, 1901–1960

Unit: 1,000 M/T

Year	Quantity of Commercial Fertilizer Consumed [a]	Index	Year	Quantity of Commercial Fertilizer Consumed [a]	Index
1901	14	100.00	1931	298	2,128.57
1902	13	92.86	1932	282	2,014.28
1903	14	100.00	1933	320	2,285.72
1904	15	107.14	1934	364	2,600.00
1905	15	107.14	1935	423	3,021.43
1906	17	121.43	1936	438	3,128.57
1907	19	135.71	1937	461	3,292.86
1908	29	207.14	1938	472	3,371.43
1909	61	435.71	1939	489	3,492.86
1910	67	478.57	1940	555	3,964.28
1911	62	442.86	1941	452	3,228.57
1912	76	542.86	1942	336	2,400.00
1913	59	421.43	1943	313	2,235.72
1914	61	435.71	1944	133	950.00
1915	84	600.00	1945	25	178.57
1916	121	864.28	1946	45	321.43
1917	145	1,035.71	1947	144	1,028.57
1918	114	814.28	1948	170	1,214.28
1919	126	900.00	1949	166	1,185.71
1920	139	992.86	1950	285	2,035.71

8. In Chapter 7, Shishido's fixed capital series and its rates of increase will be used and applied to the fixed capital series compiled here to establish an aggregate input index. The result will then be compared with the aggregate input index based upon the fixed capital series as estimated here.

TABLE 21 (Continued)

Year	Quantity of Commercial Fertilizer Consumed [a]	Index	Year	Quantity of Commercial Fertilizer Consumed [a]	Index
1921	138	985.71	1951	345	2,464.28
1922	122	871.43	1952	458	3,271.43
1923	141	1,007.14	1953	502	3,585.71
1924	176	1,257.14	1954	568	4,057.14
1925	203	1,450.00	1955	562	4,014.28
1926	213	1,521.43	1956	633	4,521.43
1927	231	1,650.00	1957	663	4,735.71
1928	261	1,864.28	1958	682	4,871.43
1929	256	1,828.57	1959	679	4,850.00
1930	265	1,892.86	1960	665	4,750.00

a. Both value and quantity of commercial fertilizers imported from Japan are known for 1914–42; data on value imported are available since 1901. On this basis, the average importing price for fertilizers is estimated. These prices are taken as the general importing price for each year. Since value of commercial fertilizers imported are known for 1901–21, quantity imported is easily obtained. Quantity of fertilizers consumed each year is the sum of quantity imported and the amount domestically produced.

Source: Value of commercial fertilizers imported for 1901–1921 taken from *Statistical Summary*, Table 327. Quantity of fertilizers imported from Japan is from N. Kayo, ed., *Basic Agricultural Statistics of Japan*, Table F-C-5. Data on the consumption of commercial fertilizers are from *Statistical Summary*, Table 211; data of fertilizer consumption for 1946–1948 taken from Taiwan, Department of Agriculture and Forestry, *Agriculture and Forestry Progress*, p. 171. Consumption of commercial fertilizers for 1949–1960 are from *Statistical Book*, 1962 edition, p. 31. Data on domestic production of commercial fertilizers are from *Statistical Summary*, Table 282.

most noticeable feature of the changes in Taiwan's agricultural inputs is the sharp and remarkable increase in commercial fertilizer inputs during the period under study. Although commercial fertilizers were first introduced to Taiwan as early as the beginning of the century, extensive use of them did not begin until the late 1930s. For the prewar period, the quantity of commercial fertilizers consumed reached the peak of 550,000 metric tons in 1940. There was then a sharp decline in the use of commercial fertilizers between 1944 and 1946. Rapid recovery took place thereafter; since 1954, the consumption of commercial fertilizers has surpassed the prewar peak. Despite the fact that Taiwan's agriculture depends heavily upon the application of fertilizers, the production of commercial fertilizers in Taiwan has been inadequate to meet the demand. Commercial fertilizer output was negligible before 1912. Although the domestic production of commercial fertilizers has increased gradually, the major source of supply is still coming from imports mainly from Japan.

Rice, sugar cane, tobacco, jute, and wheat are major fertilizer-using crops. Data on the allocation of fertilizers among different crops are not available for the prewar years. But in view of the importance of rice and sugar cane to Taiwan's agricultural economy, there is reason to believe that commercial fertilizers were largely used for the production of the two major crops during the prewar period.[9] Table 22 presents the allocation of commercial fertilizers for the postwar period. As clearly shown, the consumption of commercial fertilizers on rice and sugar cane fields during the period of 1949–1960 accounted for over 90 percent of the total.

TABLE 22

Percentage Distribution of Commercial Fertilizers,
1949–1960

Year	Rice	Sugar Cane	Tobacco	Sweet Potatoes	Jute	Wheat	Other Crops	Total
1949	60.8	37.7	—	0.4	—	0.8	0.3	100.0
1950	81.2	17.5	—	—	—	1.1	0.2	100.0
1951	81.0	15.6	—	—	0.5	1.2	1.7	100.0
1952	79.0	16.1	0.5	0.5	1.0	0.8	2.1	100.0
1953	75.3	16.8	0.8	2.1	0.7	0.7	3.6	100.0
1954	81.0	12.6	0.7	1.4	0.7	0.9	2.7	100.0
1955	78.6	14.0	1.0	0.2	1.4	1.1	3.7	100.0
1956	77.5	14.3	1.2	1.0	1.0	1.3	3.7	100.0
1957	74.3	15.7	1.2	1.1	0.7	1.6	5.4	100.0
1958	73.4	14.6	1.1	1.2	1.3	0.6	7.8	100.0
1959	73.4	14.6	1.0	0.4	1.7	1.5	7.4	100.0
1960	75.0	14.6	1.0	0.2	1.9	—	7.3	100.0

Source: Computed from data drawn from Taiwan, Economic Research Center, *Taiwan Statistical Data Book*, Table 4–9, p. 32.

9. Some 390,000 out of 472,000 metric tons of fertilizers were used on rice fields in 1938. Norton S. Ginsburg, *The Economic Resources and Development of Formosa*, p. 9.

In spite of the fact that the consumption of commercial fertilizers had steadily increased during the period of 1901–1960, farm-produced fertilizers remain important to agricultural production in Taiwan. According to a 1954 survey report of the Joint Commission on Rural Reconstruction, farmers in central Taiwan commonly applied to each acre of rice 56,000 kilograms of compost and 870 kilograms of green manure in addition to 470 kilograms of ammonium sulfate and calcium, 187 kilograms of calcium superphosphate, and 20 kilograms of potassium chloride.[10] Data are not available to make it possible to assess the long-term trend of the consumption of farm-supplied fertilizers. The supply of farm-produced fertilizers is, however, closely related to the number of humans and animals, particularly cattle and hogs. The population increased more than threefold from 3.0 million in 1901 to 10.8 million in 1960; cattle from 235,000 to 421,000 head, hogs from 701,000 to 3,165,000 head in the same period.[11] The increased population and number of animals must undoubtedly have enlarged the supply of farm-supplied fertilizers in the period.

10. Quoted in T. H. Shen, *Agricultural Planning and Production,* p. 12.

11. Cattle and hog data of 1901 are taken from *Agricultural Statistics,* p. 109; 1960 data from *Agricultural Yearbook,* 1961 edition, pp. 173–182. Population of 1901 is extrapolated from 1902 and 1903 population data in Takakoshi, *Japanese Rule in Formosa,* p. 197; 1960 data is from Taiwan, Economic Research Center, *Taiwan Statistical Data Book,* p. 4.

Chapter 6

INPUT-OUTPUT RELATIONS—CHANGES IN AGRICULTURAL PRODUCTIVITY

Productivity is a descriptive measurement relating input employed to the output produced. Specifically, productivity of a given factor is the ratio of the output produced to the given factor used. It therefore measures output per unit of input. Whereas such partial measurement of factor productivity serves a definite and useful purpose, it takes no account of other factors contributing to output. A more meaningful measure is the ratio of output to the aggregate input.

An aggregate input index has definite economic content. A particular method of aggregating input specifies a particular type of production function. A commonly used, weighted, arithmetic formula of aggregating input implies the assumption of a linear and homogeneous production function. Consider a simple two-factor case; the aggregate input index is derived from the following form:

$$I_t = \frac{i_t}{i_0} = \frac{a \cdot {}_1x_t + b \cdot {}_2x_t}{a \cdot {}_1x_0 + b \cdot {}_2x_0}$$

Define I_t as the aggregate input index relating year t to year 0; i is aggregate input, ${}_1x$ and ${}_2x$ are the two inputs in physical units; a and b are weights attached to ${}_1x$ and ${}_2x$, respectively. The method of aggregating individual inputs in any particular year therefore specifies a linear and homogeneous production function of the following form:

$$g = a(x_1) + b(x_2)$$

where g represents output.

An aggregate input index based on the geometric formula specifies a log-linear production function. Expressed in symbols as defined previously:

$$I_t = \frac{i_t}{i_0} = \frac{{}_1x_t{}^a \cdot {}_2x_t{}^b}{{}_1x_0{}^a \cdot {}_2x_0{}^b}$$

If all inputs are classified either as $_1x$ or $_2x$ and factor shares are used as weights, a and b always add up to one. This method of aggregating inputs implies a Cobb-Douglas production function:

$$g = A(x_1{}^a)(x_2{}^{1-a})$$

To define Q as output, K capital, L labor, and t time, allowing for technical change broadly defined, a dynamic production function can be written, as Professor Solow has shown, in the following form: [1]

$$Q = F(K,L; t) \tag{1}$$

In the special case when technical change is assumed to be neutral, that is, the rates of substitution of factors are not affected by shifts in the production function, the dynamic production function in the form of equation (1) can be written as:

$$Q = A(t) f(K,L) \tag{2}$$

Differentiate equation (2) with respect to time and divide by Q, the output:

$$\frac{\dot{Q}}{Q} = \frac{\dot{A}}{A} + A \cdot \frac{\partial F}{\partial K} \cdot \frac{\dot{K}}{Q} + A \cdot \frac{\partial F}{\partial L} \cdot \frac{\dot{L}}{Q} \tag{3}$$

Dots indicate time derivatives. To define a and b as $\dfrac{\partial Q}{\partial K} \cdot \dfrac{K}{Q}$, the output elasticity of capital, and $\dfrac{\partial Q}{\partial L} \cdot \dfrac{L}{Q}$, that of labor, respectively, and substitute them in equation (3), the following can be derived:

$$\frac{\dot{Q}}{Q} = \frac{\dot{A}}{A} + a\frac{\dot{K}}{K} + b\frac{\dot{L}}{L} \tag{4}$$

If factors are assumed to be paid their marginal products and the production function is assumed to be homogeneous, then by virtue of Euler's theorem, an equality exists between observed relative factor

1. Robert M. Solow, "Technical Change and the Aggregate Production Function," *Review of Economics and Statistics*, XXXIX (August 1957), pp. 312–320.

shares and the output elasticities. Using the discrete year-to-year changes as an approximation, one can rewrite equation (4) as:

$$\bar{Q} = \bar{A} + a\bar{K} + b\bar{L} \tag{5}$$

In equation (5), $\bar{Q}$, $\bar{A}$, $\bar{K}$, and $\bar{L}$ are annual rates of changes of Q, A, K, and L. With the help of observed factor shares, Solow used this form in estimating the aggregate production function of United States for the period of 1909–1949 and separating shifts in aggregate production function from movements along a given production function.

By taking the logarithms of both sides of a Cobb-Douglas production of the form:

$$Q = A \cdot K^a L^b$$

and differentiating totally with respect to time, one obtains:

$$\bar{Q} = \bar{A} + a\bar{K} + b\bar{L} \tag{6}$$

which is identical to Solow's equation as defined in equation (5). Here also the values of a and b are taken from observed factor shares.

The aggregate input index calculated here is based on the geometric formula. The following three assumptions are therefore implicitly made: (1) the aggregate production function is log-linear and homogeneous of degree one, (2) technical change is neutral, and (3) factors are paid their marginal products (i.e., the factor markets are competitive). The advantage of using a geometric formula in deriving the aggregate input is that the individual relative growth components are additive. It allows one to say how much of the rate of change in output is attributable to technical change and how much is attributable to changes in each of the inputs.

Input factors are classified into four categories: land, labor, fixed capital, and working capital. The production function implicitly assumed here takes the following form:

$$y = A \cdot x_1^a \cdot x_2^b \cdot x_3^c \cdot x_4^d$$

where y represents output; x_1, x_2, x_3, and x_4 are land, labor, working capital, and fixed capital, respectively; a, b, c, and d are weights assigned to each individual input.

If I_t is the aggregate input index of year t in relation to year 0, aggregate input index is given by the form:

$$I_t = {}_1X_t{}^{0.2462} {}_2X_t{}^{0.4524} {}_3X_t{}^{0.1929} {}_4X_t{}^{0.1085}$$

Where ${}_iX_t = {}_ix_t/{}_ix_o$ and ${}_ix_t$ stands for input i in physical units employed in year t. The exponents are weights attached to each factor, and they are factor shares in the total cost of production. Total cost of production includes imputed land rental, imputed labor cost, cost of chemical fertilizers, and interest charge on fixed capital. All factors are valued at the 1952–1956 average factor prices.[2] Total cost is calculated for a number of years evenly selected (five-year intervals). The arithmetic means of each factor cost for these selected years are taken as the weights of factors. The 1952–1956 average factor prices are chosen because the output series as compiled here uses weights by the 1952–1956 average product prices. To take both product and factor prices from the same period is to make the output and input series comparable and consistent.

The aggregate input index so compiled from the preceding formula is shown in Table 23. For comparison purpose, an aggregate input index based on the arithmetic formula is also shown in the same table. The semi-logarithmic time series chart (Figure 5) depicts the long-term changes in output, individual inputs, and the aggregate input during the period under review.

Changes in output are brought about either as a result of changes in input used or as result of technical change or both. The aggregate input index defines and indicates the expected output changes. The aggregate input index is simply the output index in the absence of technical change broadly defined. The average compound rate of increase in the ex-

2. There was a considerable change in relative factor prices during the period. Average cost of capital for 1945–1956 increased about 350 percent compared with 1935–1937, prices of commercial fertilizers increased by 100 percent, but the wage rate virtually remained the same. The implementation of the land reform during the immediate postwar years caused the fall in land rental by some 31 percent when 1945–1956 is compared with 1935–1937. See S. C. Hsieh and T. H. Lee, *An Analytical Review*, p. 42.

TABLE 23

Aggregate Input Index, 1901–1960

(Base Year: 1903)

Year	Aggregate Input Index (Geometric)	Aggregate Input Index (Arithmetic) (1952–56 factor prices)
1901	89.1	85.8
1902	92.2	90.4
1903	100.0	100.0
1904	107.4	108.8
1905	108.7	109.9
1906	112.4	111.2
1907	117.6	115.1
1908	128.9	118.2
1909	148.6	121.2
1910	156.0	124.6
1911	155.0	140.8
1912	161.5	131.0
1913	153.7	133.7
1914	154.7	134.8
1915	165.2	140.7
1916	177.8	149.3
1917	183.5	153.3
1918	175.7	145.4
1919	180.1	152.7
1920	183.4	146.9
1921	182.0	145.4
1922	176.6	142.7
1923	182.3	146.3
1924	191.8	155.3
1925	199.0	161.8
1926	202.0	164.5
1927	205.5	169.1
1928	211.9	175.0
1929	209.8	172.1
1930	213.2	177.0
1931	218.9	184.2
1932	215.4	182.6
1933	224.4	190.2
1934	233.1	200.7
1935	242.9	213.2
1936	246.7	218.5
1937	249.6	222.9
1938	252.6	224.2

TABLE 23 (Continued)

Year	Aggregate Input Index (Geometric)	Aggregate Input Index (Arithmetic) (1952–56 factor prices)
1939	255.4	223.5
1940	257.3	236.2
1941	249.0	221.9
1942	236.7	202.3
1943	234.6	197.2
1944	195.9	165.7
1945	139.6	136.7
1946	157.5	149.7
1947	197.5	176.6
1948	210.7	188.1
1949	213.7	192.1
1950	238.7	216.4
1951	250.4	229.0
1952	265.1	246.3
1953	270.2	256.1
1954	281.0	272.5
1955	277.0	267.3
1956	282.6	281.1
1957	285.1	287.7
1958	288.3	295.0
1959	288.6	293.9
1960	294.3	308.2

Source: See the text.

pected aggregate output comes to 2.0 percent per year. During the period from 1901 to 1960, land input increased at the rate of 1.4 percent per year, labor input 0.6 percent, working capital 6.6 percent, and fixed capital 1.0 percent. Of the 2.0 percent annual rate of increase, 0.34 percent is caused by the increase in land area, 0.27 percent by labor, 0.11 percent by fixed capital, and 1.27 percent by working capital.[3] The observed rate of increase in the agricultural output during the whole period is 3.14 percent (compound) a year. The discrepancy of 1.14 percent between the observed and expected rate of increase in agricultural output represents the contribution of technical change broadly defined.

3. The sum of the four is 1.99; 2.0 results from rounding.

Figure 5

INDICES OF OUTPUT, AGGREGATE INPUT, AND INDIVIDUAL INPUTS

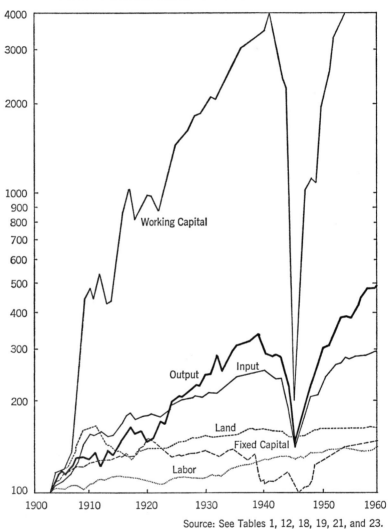

Source: See Tables 1, 12, 18, 19, 21, and 23.

Based on the aggregate input and output series compiled here, changes in input productivity can be calculated by dividing the aggregate input index into the output index. The results are presented in Table 24. Productivity of the aggregate input increased about 60 percent

TABLE 24 [a]

Index of Factor Productivity

(*1903* = *100*)

Period	Aggregate Input	Land	Labor	Fixed Capital
1901–1905	96.7	102.3	96.5	95.6
1906–1910	95.9	102.6	120.4	87.1
1911–1915	85.9	104.6	122.6	90.9
1916–1920	86.6	114.0	140.2	112.9
1921–1925	96.8	127.1	165.8	130.9
1926–1930	107.2	148.8	200.3	165.0
1931–1935	120.8	178.4	235.1	204.0
1936–1940	126.8	197.4	251.9	262.1
1941–1945	114.1	154.8	186.5	220.2
1946–1950	111.6	143.3	170.8	201.2
1951–1955	133.5	219.6	257.6	260.7
1956–1960	159.8	280.6	330.5	315.0

a. (1) Note that bases of all input indices and output have been shifted from 1901 to 1903. (2) Productivity of working capital is not computed here: the working capital index increased too rapidly largely because of the initially small basis.

Source: Computed from Tables 1, 12, 18, 19, and 23.

during the 1901–1960 period. Instead of spreading evenly over the whole period, increase in productivity was very much concentrated in the two periods of 1926–1940 and 1951–1960 (see Figure 6). There was no significant change in productivity between the years of 1901 and 1925. The index of factor productivity in 1921–1925 was practically the same as in 1901–1905. Actually, there was a noticeable decline in agricultural productivity between 1911 and 1920. Improvement in agricultural production is noticeable in the latter part of the third decade of the century when productivity rose by 10 percent in the period of 1926–1930 in comparison with 1921–1925. A more rapid rise in productivity took place in the period of 1926–1930, when productivity showed another 13-percent increase as compared to its preceding period. The rate of increase in agricultural productivity declined to a moderate 5 percent between 1931–1935 and 1936–1940. The period of 1951–1960 showed the most rapid increase in productivity: an impressively high rate of 4 percent per year had been attained and maintained during this period.

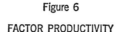

Figure 6

FACTOR PRODUCTIVITY

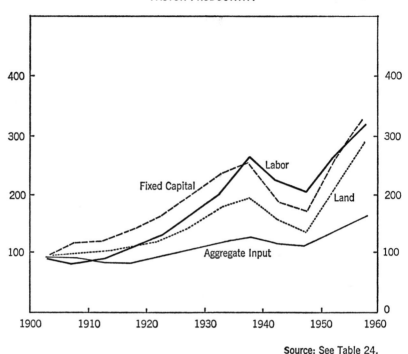

Source: See Table 24.

The pattern of individual factor productivity change is very similar to that of the aggregate input productivity. During the entire period, land productivity rose by 180 percent, labor productivity by 230 percent, and fixed capital productivity by 215 percent. As in the case of aggregate input productivity, all these improvements were mainly achieved in the two periods of 1926–1940 and 1951–1960.

To explain how an agriculture of low productivity can be transformed into a highly productive one, Professor T. W. Schultz proposes the "price of permanent income streams" hypothesis.[4] He views economic growth as equivalent to an increase in the number of income streams.

4. *Transforming Traditional Agriculture.*

In his words,

a useful way of looking at economic growth is to identify the different sources of income streams and to determine the price at which each of the respective sources can be increased.[5]

The price of these income streams can be determined, as any other prices, by demand and supply.

The demanders are the owners of capital who buy the sources of income streams in order to acquire the income from them; the suppliers are the enterprises or persons who produce the sources of permanent income streams with a view to selling them.[6]

In an agriculture where the state of arts and the state of preference and motives for acquiring additional sources of income streams remain constant and both of the states remain constant long enough to allow the marginal productivity of investment and net savings to approach zero, a peculiar type of equilibrium of stagnation is obtained. Schultz defines it as the traditional agriculture.[7] The important attribute of this traditional agriculture is that production is wholly based on traditional factors. A traditional agriculture is efficient but poor according to Schultz because there are few significant inefficiencies of allocation of factors.[8] Reallocation of resources and an increase in investment restricted to the traditional factors will not improve production possibilities. Farmers' lack of incentives to invest and to save in traditional agriculture where reproducible capital is alleged to be scarce often seems to be a puzzle. The economic explanation of this behavior is that the price of acquiring additional sources of income is too high or that the rate of return to investment is too low.[9] Agriculture will remain niggardly and unable to contribute to economic growth so long as there are only traditional factors at its disposal. The essential attribute of a traditional agriculture is the constant state of arts which conditions the supply function of the sources of permanent income streams. When the supply function shifts downward, farmers have the incentive to demand additional sources of income. This resulting increase in investment breaks the long-run equilibrium of stagnation. The cheap sources of permanent income streams

5. *Ibid.*, p. 75.
6. *Ibid.*, p. 76.
7. *Ibid.*, p. 29.
8. *Ibid.*, p. 3.
9. *Ibid.*, p. 84.

can be realized only if new nontraditional factors are introduced and farmers are equipped with the skill to utilize them. The important implication of Schultz's hypothesis is that investment in agriculture restricted to the traditional type of inputs is a source of economic growth subject to increasing costs. Stagnation is inevitable in the long run unless new inputs appear on the scene.

According to the input package employed, Taiwan's agricultural development during the period under review can be divided into three distinctive subperiods. During the first twenty years of the period, increased agricultural output was brought about mainly by additions to the traditional inputs—land, labor, and fixed capital. The succeeding period from 1921 to 1940 was one of transition with incremental input package being characterized by a mixture of traditional and nontraditional factors. Output increases in the period of 1946–1960 resulted from a reliance on nontraditional inputs. The initial emphasis on acreage expansion would probably suggest that this had been a cheap source of growth at the outset relative to other alternatives. As in the case of Taiwan in the first subperiod, early reliance on increased use of traditional factors for sources of growth was common to many other agricultures. Acreage expansion initially was also the principal source of growth in the United States, and until about 1919 resource productivity in U. S. agriculture fell.[10] So long as forms of investment in agriculture remain traditional, the rate of return on investment eventually falls, as it did, to the point where alternatives using new inputs become decidedly more attractive. And if new inputs do not appear, agriculture reaches the peculiar type of equilibrium described by Schultz—long-run stagnation then prevails. That state probably would have been reached some time in the second subperiod in the case of Taiwan. Because of alert policy-making, actions were taken shifting emphasis from further land clearing to yield-increasing forms of investment. This observed evolutionary change and the eventual pre-eminence of the new, nontraditional inputs on Taiwan's agricultural scene supports Schultz's contention that over a long period of time, continual infusion of new inputs are necessary to sustain growth in agriculture.

10. See John W. Kendrick, *Productivity Trends in the United States,* Table B–I, pp. 362–364.

Chapter 7

THE RESIDUAL AND ITS CONTRIBUTING
FACTORS: I

Changes in input productivity are a result of the disparity between input and output increment. If the aggregate production function is truly homogeneous of degree one and remains unchanged over time, the changes in output must be fully accounted for by the changes in inputs employed. The aggregate output index can then be representative of the aggregate input index and vice versa. During the period 1901–1960, land input increased at an average rate of 1.4 percent per year, labor input 0.6 percent, working capital input 6.6 percent, and fixed capital input 1.0 percent. Increase in the aggregate input is at an average rate of 2.0 percent per year. Thus, the rate of growth in agricultural output is also expected to be 2.0 percent per year. However, the actual growth of farm output during the period is measured at a rate of 3.14 percent. The difference between the actual and the expected rate of growth in farm output is attributed to "technical change."

As has been shown in the previous chapter, take the logarithms of both sides of a Cobb-Douglas production function:

$$Q = A \cdot K^a \cdot L^b$$

and differentiate with respect to time; the following is obtained:

$$\bar{Q} = \bar{A} + a\bar{K} + b\bar{L}$$

The rate of change in output is the sum of the rate of technical change broadly defined and the rates of change on capital and labor inputs weighted by the factor shares, respectively. Recall that the assumed production function here takes the following form:

$$y = A \cdot x_1{}^a \cdot x_2{}^b \cdot x_3{}^c \cdot x_4{}^d$$

Write $\bar{Y}$ as the rate of change in output and $\bar{A}$ as the rate of technical change, $\bar{X}_1$, $\bar{X}_2$, $\bar{X}_3$, and $\bar{X}_4$ as the rates of change in land input, labor input, working capital input, and fixed capital input, respectively, and *a, b, c,* and *d* are the weights assigned to land, labor, working capital, and fixed capital, respectively:

$$\bar{Y} = \bar{A} + a\bar{X}_1 + b\bar{X}_2 + c\bar{X}_3 + d\bar{X}_4$$

From this equation, it appears that of the 3.14-percent annual increase in farm output during the period, 36.4 percent (1.14 of 3.14 percent) is attributable to technical change, which is defined here as a shorthand expression for the factors that are yet to be identified, 10.9 percent (0.34 of 3.14 percent) attributable to the increase in land input, 8.6 percent (0.27 of 3.14 percent) to the increase in labor input, 40.6 percent (1.27 of 3.14 percent) to working capital, and 3.5 percent (0.11 of 3.14 percent) to the increased use of fixed capital.

The discrepancy between the observed and the expected rate of growth in farm output suggests that a linearly homogeneous production function based on input classified in the traditional manner is poorly specified and does not adequately represent the true aggregate production function in a dynamic setting. That is to say, the implicit production function assumed in the previous chapter cannot have the form:

$$y_t = A \cdot {}_1x_t{}^a \cdot {}_2x_t{}^b \cdot {}_3x_t{}^c \cdot {}_4x_t{}^d \tag{1}$$

Instead, equation (1) must be written as:

$$y_t = A(t) \cdot {}_1x_t{}^a \cdot {}_2x_t{}^b \cdot {}_3x_t{}^c \cdot {}_4x_t{}^d \tag{2}$$

where $A(t)$ measures the contribution of technical change to output. Let r be the rate of technical change in discrete approximation. Equation (2) can be rewritten as:

$$y_t = A(1+r)^t \cdot {}_1x_t{}^a \cdot {}_2x_t{}^b \cdot {}_3x_t{}^c \cdot {}_4x_t{}^d$$

As defined in Chapter 6, $G_t = y_t/y_o$ and $_iX_t = {}_ix_t/{}_ix_o$ and hence,

$$G_t = y_t/y_0 = (1+r)^t \cdot {}_1X_t{}^a \cdot {}_2X_t{}^b \cdot {}_3X_t{}^c \cdot {}_4X_t{}^d$$

But ${}_1X_t{}^a \cdot {}_2X_t{}^b \cdot {}_3X_t{}^c \cdot {}_4X_t{}^d = I_t$; thus there results:

$$G_t = (1+r)^t \cdot I_t \tag{3}$$

Define G_{ct} as the expected output index, and in the absence of technical change $G_{ct} = I_t$. The difference between the two, multiplied by the output of the base year, y_0, measures the part of the observed output that is left unexplained by the conventional inputs. Expressed in symbols:

$$y'_t = G_t \cdot y_0 - G_{ct} \cdot y_0 = G_t \cdot y_0 - I_t \cdot y_0 \qquad (4)$$

Since $G_t = y_t/y_0$, equation (4) can be rewritten as:

$$y'_t = y_t - I_t \cdot y_0 \qquad (5)$$

From equation (5) the output series attributable to technical change, defined as y'_t, can be calculated; the rate of technical change r can be obtained from equation (3). The results are given in Tables 25 and 26.

The appearance of the negative computed unexplained output between 1909 and 1923 seems to be a puzzle. Nevertheless, the period under review is not a homogeneous one in view of the input package employed as noted in the previous chapter. During the first two decades of the period, agricultural production was almost wholly based on the traditional factors. Increase in farm output was brought about by the increased use of services of land, labor, current input, and fixed capital input. The state of arts in agriculture remained very much unchanged. The appearance of the negative unexplained output is indicative of the diminishing return and the niggardliness of nature in a traditional agriculture. Insofar as the land input is measured by land area, the quality of land is implicitly taken to be constant. The negative unexplained output could therefore be interpreted in terms of Ricardo's rent theory: the quality of newly cultivated land is inferior.

Professor Anthony M. Tang suggests six factors that may be responsible for the computed (positive) unexplained output: [1] (1) the aggregate production function is not strictly linear—not linearly homogeneous in the present case—, (2) technology in a strict sense has changed, (3) the factor price weights of the input index were not taken from a

1. Anthony M. Tang, "Research and Education."

TABLE 25

Observed, Expected, and "Unexplained" Output

(*Unit: millions of NT$*)

Year	Observed Output [a] y_t	Expected Output $(I_t \cdot y_0)$	Unexplained Output [b] (equation 5)
1903	1,959.6	1,959.6	0
1904	2,193.6	2,104.6	89.0
1905	2,318.3	2,130.1	188.2
1906	2,231.3	2,202.6	28.7
1907	2,423.9	2,304.5	119.4
1908	2,547.7	2,525.9	21.8
1909	2,595.8	2,912.0	−316.2
1910	2,533.3	3,057.0	−523.7
1911	2,676.2	3,037.4	−361.2
1912	2,408.0	3,164.8	−756.8
1913	2,739.2	3,011.9	−272.7
1914	2,622.9	3,031.5	−408.6
1915	2,840.4	3,237.2	−396.8
1916	2,981.4	3,484.2	−502.8
1917	3,244.2	3,595.9	−351.7
1918	3,063.3	3,443.0	−379.7
1919	3,104.0	3,529.2	−425.2
1920	2,883.6	3,593.9	−710.3
1921	3,032.1	3,566.3	−534.4
1922	3,396.8	3,460.6	− 63.8
1923	3,304.2	3,572.4	−268.2
1924	3,877.4	3,758.5	118.9
1925	4,096.0	3,899.6	196.4
1926	4,020.1	3,958.4	61.7
1927	4,245.6	4,027.0	218.6
1928	4,428.4	4,152.4	276.0
1929	4,450.4	4,111.2	339.2
1930	4,766.0	4,177.9	588.1
1931	4,873.4	4,289.6	583.8
1932	5,586.1	4,221.0	1,365.1
1933	5,031.0	4,397.3	633.7
1934	5,484.3	4,567.8	916.5
1935	5,884.6	4,759.9	1,124.7
1936	6,114.2	4,834.3	1,279.9
1937	6,199.5	4,891.2	1,308.3
1938	6,489.2	4,949.9	1,539.3
1939	6,553.7	5,004.8	1,548.9
1940	5,641.4	5,042.0	599.4

TABLE 25 (Continued)

Year	Observed Output [a] y_t	Expected Output $(I_t \cdot y_0)$	Unexplained Output [b] (*equation 5*)
1941	5,563.8	4,879.4	684.4
1942	5,639.5	4,638.4	1,001.1
1943	5,385.9	4,597.2	788.7
1944	4,540.9	3,838.8	702.1
1945	2,721.8	2,735.6	− 13.8
1946	3,127.1	3,086.4	40.7
1947	3,767.1	3,870.2	−103.1
1948	4,478.4	4,128.9	349.5
1949	5,221.7	4,187.7	1,034.0
1950	5,905.5	4,677.6	1,227.9
1951	6,085.6	4,906.8	1,178.8
1952	6,649.5	5,194.9	1,454.6
1953	7,480.0	5,294.8	2,185.2
1954	7,508.7	5,506.5	2,002.2
1955	7,480.8	5,428.1	2,052.7
1956	8,144.4	5,537.8	2,606.6
1957	8,867.2	5,586.8	3,280.4
1958	9,402.3	5,649.5	3,752.8
1959	9,331.2	5,655.4	3,675.8
1960	9,338.9	5,767.1	3,571.8

a. $y_0 = NT\$ 1959.6$ million
b. Because of the abnormality in the first two years of the period, the base has been shifted to 1903. 1901 and 1902 are omitted; by definition the unexplained output in the base year, 1903, is equal to zero.
Source: The observed output series is taken from Table 3; input index from Table 23.

competitive setting, (4) the quality of labor has changed, (5) general economic efficiency has improved, and (6) the degree with which resources are utilized has changed.

If the aggregate production function is not linearly homogeneous, the derivation of the aggregate input index based on the geometric formula (a Cobb-Douglas production function is implicitly assumed) will undoubtedly lead to a computed unexplained output. Whether the aggregate production function is truly homogeneous of degree one and how changes in farm scale will affect the farm output are empirical ques-

TABLE 26

Rates of Technical Progress

Period	Rate of Technical Progress (Compound Rate)
1901–1910	−0.4
1911–1920	−0.9
1921–1930	2.9
1931–1940	−0.2
(1931–1939)	1.6
1941–1950	1.1
1951–1960	2.7
1901–1960	1.1
1901–1939	1.1
1946–1960	3.2
1952–1960	2.6

Source: The rate of technical progress is computed from the formula: $G_t = (1 + r)^t \cdot I_t$; see the text.

tions. The relationship between size and economic efficiency is meaningful only if the techniques of production are specified. Large farms are not necessarily more efficient than small farms. As Schultz argues, in traditional agriculture returns are likely to be quite independent of scale. Growth of agriculture cannot be realized by changing the scale of operation alone.[2] Even if farm size and efficiency of farm operation are assumed to be correlated, the effect of the changes in farm scale upon agricultural output has probably been small in Taiwan because of the small and insignificant change in farm scale during the period 1901–1960. The average farm size increased from 1.60 hectare per farm household to 2.0 hectares per farm household between 1901 and 1940 (see Table 27). The average farm size declined, however, between 1940 and 1960 from 2.0 hectares to 1.20 hectare. Data on the distribution of farm sizes are not available before 1920. Changes in the distribution of farm sizes between 1920 and 1960 are known and recorded in the reports of farm surveys of 1920, 1932, 1939, and 1956.[3] They reveal that there

2. Theodore W. Schultz, *Transforming Traditional Agriculture*, p. 111.
3. Data of 1920, 1932, and 1939 are in *Statistical Summary*, Table 199, pp. 528–531; data of 1956 in *Report on 1956 Sample Census*, p. 1.

TABLE 27

Farm Size, 1901–1960

Period	Average Farm Size (Hectare)
1901–1910	1.60 [a]
1911–1920	1.81 [a]
1921–1930	1.97
1931–1940	2.00
1941–1950	1.62
1951–1960	1.20

a. The number of farm households for 1901–1920 is not available. The figures are estimated by dividing the trend values of average persons per household into the agricultural population. The average size is then obtained by dividing the land area by the number of farm households so estimated.

Source: For land area see Table 18; data on the number of farm households from *Agricultural Statistics*, p. 8, and *Agricultural Yearbook* 1961 edition, p. 24.

was a tendency toward concentration in holdings between 1920 and 1939; a reverse change in the distribution of farm size, as shown in the decline of the number of small farms, took place between 1939 and 1956 (see Table 28). Nevertheless, the changes in land distribution and farm size are relatively small and insignificant throughout the period. The manner in which agriculture of Taiwan is organized is characterized by the small-size farming on the family basis. Farms with sizes under 2.0 chias—equivalent to 1.94 hectares—are predominant during the whole period.

The derived aggregate input index is undoubtedly sensitive to the weights used. A computed unexplained output could result from the use of factor prices as weights that are not taken from a competitive setting. Although the matter of weighting is important, one cannot rigorously test if the computed "unexplained" output is a result of the departure of factor prices from their respective marginal productivities. The best one can do is to derive the factor weights according to some clearly defined criteria. In the present case, the factor weights are estimated from the 1952–1956 average factor prices. Compared in retrospect, the factor weights derived from the 1952–1956 average prices are close to the relative factor weights in Japan based on Shishido's 1933–1937 values of agricultural input.[4] In Japan, land service accounted for 26.1 percent, labor service 51.5 percent, current input 14.2 percent, and capital service 8.2 percent. The relative weights of inputs in Taiwan are—land: 24.62 percent; labor: 45.24 percent; working capital: 19.29 percent; and fixed capital: 10.85 percent. It is reassuring to find the Japanese and Taiwan sets of weights so similar because the conditions that then governed the agricultural production in the two countries were similar. However, this is not to imply that the Japanese weights should be used as a standard.

TABLE 28

Percentage Distribution of Farm Size, Selected Years

Year	Under 0.5 chia [a]	Above 0.5, Under 1 chia	Above 1 chia Under 2 chia	Above 2 chia	Total
1920	30.3	22.9	23.7	23.1	100.0
1932	24.3	20.2	25.8	29.7	100.0
1939	25.6	20.6	25.9	27.9	100.0
1956 [b]	34.4	28.4	25.5	11.7	100.0

a. 1 chia is equivalent to 0.96992 hectare.
b. The noncultivator category is omitted.
Source: Data of 1920, 1932, and 1939 computed from data drawn from *Statistical Summary*, Table 199, pp. 528–531; 1956 figure computed from *Report on the 1956 Sample Census*, Table 1, p. 1.

Better transportation facilities, public health conditions, and general institutional frameworks will improve efficiency of agricultural production. Although they are important to agricultural production, the effects of these variables upon farm output are not assessable statistically. The treatment of the effects of those variables upon the unexplained output is therefore confined to broad terms.

The sharp increase in agricultural output during the period of 1901–1960 is accompanied by an impressive improvement in transportation facilities, public health conditions, and other broad socio-economic set-

4. Quoted in Tang, "Research and Education," p. 93.

tings. Immediately after Taiwan was annexed to Japan in 1895 and the Japanese campaign against the revolt for independence was ended successfully, the new authority wasted no time in launching programs to improve the transportation system, to ameliorate public health conditions, and to teach the natives the Japanese language. These programs were primarily devices to consolidate the Japanese rule over Taiwan, the first colony ever acquired by Japan, rather than to improve the economic performance of Taiwan. As a by-product, however, they furnished a solid foundation for the Japanese to implement other direct projects

TABLE 29

Increase in Roads, Selected Years

Year	Road Length [a]	Index
1899	6,734	100.0
1900	6,910	102.6
1910	12,135	180.2
1920	12,322	183.0
1930	15,101	224.2
1940	—	—
1950	—	—
1960	16,229	241.0

a. Figures rounded.
Source: Data for 1899–1930 from *Statistical Summary*, Table 450, for 1960 from *Statistical Book*, Table 6–3.

later which would tap economic resources of Taiwan. The main railroad line, running on the western part of the island from north to south, was completed as early as 1908. Public roads increased rapidly between 1899 and 1910 (see Table 29). Although additions were continually made in later years, a basic but adequate transportation system had been already well established in the first decade of the century. Together with the establishment of other modern communication facilities, they probably had made a major inroad against agrarian traditionalism.

Taiwan's public health conditions in the earlier years of the period were in an extremely poor state because of the subtropical climate upon which various diseases feed and poor sanitary facilities. Tropical dysen-

tery prevailed and malaria was ordinarily endemic. In addition, Taiwan
was repeatedly attacked by plague and cholera in epidemic proportions.
The Japanese put forth great efforts to control those diseases and to
promote general sanitary conditions during the early years of their
occupation of Taiwan. Their campaign against disease and toward
improving public health conditions was a great success. Plague has

TABLE 30

Death Rates and Infant Mortality Rates, Selected Years

Period	Death Rate (Deaths per 1,000)	Infant Mortality Rate [a]
1901–1910	33.4	170
1911–1915	28.6	169
1916–1920	31.0	173
1921–1925	25.0	165
1926–1930	22.1	—
1931–1935	21.2	152
1936–1940	20.6	140
1941–1943	18.5	124
1947–1950	14.3	35
1951–1955	9.5	34
1956–1960	7.4	30

a. Figures are end years of each period. Infant mortality
rates for prewar years are unweighted means for both sexes;
Barclay's figures were used for this purpose.
Source: For 1901–1943 data taken from George W. Barclay, *Colonial Development*, Tables 36 and 39; for 1947–1960,
from S. C. Hsu, "Report on Rural Health Program in Taiwan, Republic of China," Table 3.

been completely eradicated since 1917, and cholera since 1920 has
ceased to be a threat to the populace.[5] Improvement in health conditions had been substantial throughout the period. This is clearly shown
in the persistent and rather sharp decline in infant mortality and the
crude death rate of the population (see Table 30).

The Chinese civil household organization, known as the Pao-Chia

5. Formosa Education Association, *Modern Formosa,* p. 26; see also George W.
Barclay, *Colonial Development,* pp. 136–139.

system, was first introduced to Taiwan by the Japanese as a form of police control over the native inhabitants.[6] The system was later utilized by the Japanese as an effective medium to supplement agricultural organizations in disseminating information and new techniques of production. The establishment and expansion of farmers' associations, irrigation associations, credit co-operatives, and marketing associations all functioned as avenues of communication that blanketed the rural areas. The full utilization of those rural organizations enabled the authorities in Taiwan to implement, control, and supervise effectively their agricultural improvement programs with moderate outlays. Other institutional changes occurred during the period of 1901–1960 that probably had also contributed to the general improvement in economic efficiency. The successive censuses taken during the period probably had furnished the authorities with the details of the economic potentials. A comprehensive land survey was made and completed before 1905. A large-scale reform program to regulate the tenure system, primarily for tax-collecting purposes, was implemented successfully before 1910. This reform program greatly simplified the extremely complicated and sometimes discordant tenure system existing before; it also stabilized the relationships between tenants and their landlords. Another large-scale land reform program to reduce land rental and to equalize land ownership was implemented in 1949 and completed in 1952 under the Chinese administration. All of these changes in the institutional arrangements in agriculture and in the economy at large probably had profoundly changed the economic organization of Taiwan's agriculture.

Recall that the fixed capital series as estimated and presented in Chapter 5 has shown an improbable trend. The fixed capital input series contains serious defects because of its narrow coverage. To assess how the aggregate input index has been affected and how much the computed unexplained output has been a result of narrow coverage in the fixed capital series, an aggregate input index based on the rate of increase in the fixed capital input in Japan for the period of 1900 to 1940, as estimated by Shishido, is calculated and presented in Table 31. As is expected, the difference between the two input indices is rather

6. For a brief but adequate description of the Pao-Chia system see Barclay, *ibid.*, pp. 50–52.

small; accordingly, the imperfection of the fixed capital input series as estimated could not have been important to the computed unexplained output.

TABLE 31

Aggregate Input Indices, Selected Years

(1903 = 100)

Year	Aggregate Input Index I [a]	Aggregate Input Index II [b]
1905	108.7	106.5
1910	156.0	148.9
1915	165.2	161.8
1920	183.4	180.1
1925	199.0	199.0
1930	210.9	214.7
1935	242.9	247.9
1940	257.3	275.9

a. The index contains land area, labor, working capital, and the fixed capital as estimated here.

b. The components of the input index included: land area, labor, working capital, and the fixed capital using Shishido's quinquennial data for Japan. The middle year of each period is represented here.

Source: For Shishido's fixed capital series, see Shishido, "Japanese Agriculture," Table 1.

Chapter 8

THE RESIDUAL AND ITS CONTRIBUTING
FACTORS: II

From the discussion in the previous chapter, it is now apparent by implication that the disparity between the increments in input and output during the period of 1901–1960 is to be explained in terms of changes in technology, in the quality of labor, and in the degree of resource utilization. This chapter will be devoted to a discussion of the relative importance of each of these three factors in contributing to the computed unexplained output.

The sharp and remarkable increases in crop area and the multiple-cropping index underscore the importance to Taiwan's agricultural development of increasing degree of land utilization during the period under review. Growth in farm output, however, would not have been possible at such a rapid rate had there been no considerable improvement in yield per unit of land. Index of crop yield per unit of physical land area increased 170 percent (taking the 1901–1905 period as the base) during the entire period—100 percent between 1901 and 1940, and another 70 percent between 1940 and 1960. This achievement was largely made in the two periods of 1920–1940 and 1950–1960 (see Table 32). The rapid increase in the yield per unit of physical land area is partially a result of the increased frequency of land utilization per unit of time and partially a result of the continual improvement in crop yield per unit of crop area. Taking the period as a whole, index of yield per unit of crop area increased nearly 80 percent. In contrast with the case of yield per unit of physical land area, this 80-percent betterment of yield per unit of crop area was accomplished in the span of twenty years between 1920 and 1940. Yield per unit of crop area declined during the 1941–1950 period in comparison with the preceding period; a quick recovery of crop yield took place between the years of 1951 and 1960. However, yield per unit of crop area in 1956–1960 did not quite reach the level of 1936–1940. This clearly indicates that the rapid increase in

TABLE 32

Index of Crop Yield, 1901–1960

Period	Output,[a] Millions of NT$	Crop Area			Land Area		
		Crop Area, Hectare	Yield per Hectare, NT$	Index	Land Area, Hectare	Yield per Hectare, NT$	Index
1901–1905	1,630.6	592,813	2,750.6	100.0	519,466	3,139.0	100.0
1906–1910	2,110.6	733,227	2,878.5	104.6	654,832	3,223.1	102.7
1911–1915	2,254.1	799,030	2,821.0	102.6	692,272	3,256.1	103.7
1916–1920	2,580.3	837,105	3,082.4	112.1	731,288	3,528.4	112.4
1921–1925	2,995.6	881,606	3,397.9	123.5	758,538	3,949.2	125.8
1926–1930	3,722.4	946,582	3,932.5	143.0	800,917	4,647.7	148.1
1931–1935	4,599.7	1,045,892	4,397.9	159.9	820,305	5,607.3	178.6
1936–1940	5,336.9	1,091,215	4,890.8	177.8	856,108	6,233.9	198.6
1941–1945	4,298.7	1,044,716	4,114.7	149.6	837,029	5,135.7	163.6
1946–1950	4,142.1	1,261,325	3,283.9	119.4	852,911	4,856.4	154.7
1951–1955	5,963.2	1,469,082	4,059.1	147.6	873,962	6,823.2	217.4
1956–1960	7,397.0	1,538,214	4,808.8	174.8	875,897	8,445.1	269.0

a. Output of livestock and poultry products not included. All products are valued at the 1952–1956 average farm prices.

Source: Output series taken from Table 3. For crop area, see Table 17; for land area see Table 18.

yield per unit of physical land area in the postwar period is entirely a result of the increased degree of land utilization during the period.

Rice, sugar cane, sweet potatoes, peanuts, and tea are five leading crops of Taiwan in terms of value produced and area planted. Eighty to 90 percent of the total crop area was planted with these five major crops, and they also accounted for 80 to 90 percent of the total farm output exclusive of livestock and poultry products. Therefore, yield per unit of crop area for the five major crops is decisive in determining the yield per

TABLE 33

Indices of Yields for Five Major Crops and for All Other Crops

Period	Five Major Crops	All Other Crops
1901–1905	100.0	100.0
1906–1910	105.6	97.3
1911–1915	105.5	8.5
1916–1920	114.8	92.0
1921–1925	123.3	125.4
1926–1930	141.8	153.2
1931–1935	158.0	175.7
1936–1940	178.2	172.5
1941–1945	150.5	141.3
1946–1950	118.1	122.5
1951–1955	150.4	129.9
1956–1960	178.9	152.3

Source: See Table 32.

unit of crop area for all crops. As is expected, index of crop yield for all farm products moved very closely with the index of yields for the five leading crops. Yield per unit of crop area for products other than the major five has not steadily risen during the period. In fact, it declined between the years 1906 and 1920, and the recovery of crop yield for products included in this category has not been as much as that of the leading five crops in the period of 1956–1960 (see Table 33). The average yield per unit of crop area for the five leading crops in the period of 1956–1960 nevertheless has surpassed the peak level attained in the prewar period. The fall in the average yield for all crops other than the *five* major ones is therefore responsible for the low overall yield in

1956–1960 in comparison with 1936–1940. Recall that yield per unit of physical land area is 35 percent higher in the postwar years (1956–1960) than the yield per unit of physical land area for all crops in the period of 1936–1940.[1] A possible change is indicated here in the pattern of technical advancement between the prewar and postwar periods. Whereas the growth experience in the postwar period is heavily tied to increased

TABLE 34

Indices of Yields for Rice, Sugar Cane, Sweet Potatoes, Peanuts, and Tea, 1901–1960

Period	Rice	Sugar Cane	Sweet Potatoes	Peanuts	Tea [a]
1901–1905	100.0	100.0	100.0	100.0	—
1906–1910	102.9	109.5	112.0	115.3	—
1911–1915	103.7	83.0	108.6	98.0	100.0 [b]
1916–1920	108.7	105.8	115.4	121.6	82.6
1921–1925	117.5	119.2	133.4	146.4	69.3
1926–1930	127.1	190.3	159.7	160.6	61.2
1931–1935	142.4	235.1	177.3	169.5	55.8
1936–1940	154.3	238.2	188.8	177.4	68.8
1941–1945	130.3	194.1	155.1	120.0	45.6
1946–1950	123.5	132.1	138.2	132.2	54.7
1951–1955	159.0	217.4	151.1	133.3	72.6
1956–1960	186.7	262.8	194.8	173.4	80.9

a. Note that the base for tea has been shifted to 1915 for data on yield are not available for 1901–1914.

b. 1915 only.

Source: Computed from data taken from *Agricultural Statistics;* data for 1956–1960 from *Agricultural Yearbook*, 1961 edition.

degree of land utilization, technical change in the prewar period primarily took the form of raising crop yield per unit of crop area. Of these five major crops, all but tea have shown significant improvement in yields during the prewar period. Yield of sugar cane per hectare had increased more than 160 percent during the whole period, yield of rice 87 percent, sweet potatoes 100 percent, and peanuts 75 percent (see Table 34). Yields per unit of crop area for rice, sugar cane, and sweet potatoes in the period of 1951–1960 are higher than in the prewar years.

1. The index of 198.6 for the period 1936–1940 divided into 269.0 of the period 1956–1960; see Table 32.

The rises in yields per unit of crop area were made possible through the improvement in irrigation facilities, the increasing use of chemical fertilizers, changes in farm practices, and varietal improvement in seeds. The increased application of commercial fertilizers and the varietal improvement in seeds were probably of overwhelming importance. The increases in rice yield per unit of crop area reflected the contribution of varietal improvement in seeds to the increased yield per unit of land. Increases in rice yield were relatively small before 1920; the index of rice yield per hectare rose slowly from 100.0 to 108.7. But it climbed rapidly to 117.5 in 1921–1925. The breakthrough resulted from the successful development and introduction of the hybrid varieties known as Polai rice in 1922.[2] These Polai varieties are 40 percent more productive on an experimental basis than are the native varieties known as Chailai rice.[3] Although yields per hectare for the Polai varieties declined greatly when they were adopted on farms, yield per hectare of this hybrid rice is still 10 to 20 percent higher than the native varieties.[4] The overall increase in rice yield per unit of crop area is in part the result of the expansion of area planted in Polai rice; the area planted in Polai has gradually increased from 4.4 percent of the total rice field in 1922–1925 to 47 percent in 1936–1940 and 60 percent in 1956–1960.[5] The selection of superior native rice varieties to replace inferior native varieties also raised rice yield per crop area from 1,358 kilograms per hectare in 1901–1905 to 1,870 kilograms in 1936–1940 and further to 2,343 kilograms in 1956–1960 for Chailai rice.[6] As in the case of rice, the development and introduction of improved and more productive cane varieties contributed to the increase in cane yield and sugar production. The cane varieties planted in the earlier years of the period, known as bamboo cane, produced 29,000 kilograms of cane per hectare on the average with a low sugar cane ratio of 7.44 percent. An improved cane variety known as rose cane, introduced to Taiwan in the following decade, increased the sugar cane ratio to 9.9 percent, a 20-percent improvement,

2. See Bruce F. Johnston, "Agricultural Development."
3. *Ibid.*
4. *Food Statistics Book,* pp. 18–21. Johnston had reported, ". . . this replacement of inferior native with superior native varieties raised yields by 10 to 30 percent, although the increased yield indicated by the over-all crop statistics was small," see Johnston, *op. cit.*
5. *Food Statistics Book,* pp. 4–7.
6. See Johnston, *op. cit.,* and *Food Statistics Book.*

although cane yield for this newly improved variety was lower than the yields of bamboo cane. The most notable development in introducing better varieties of cane was the successful transplanting of the POJ varieties, originally developed in Java, to Taiwan. The most productive POJ varieties were POJ 2725, POJ 2883, and POJ 2878; the average yields for those POJ varieties were 67,000 kilograms per hectare. The POJ cane varieties had a high sugar cane ratio of 13.3 percent. The further rise in cane yield in 1951–1960 again was made possible through the introduction of a better cane variety known as Nico 310 which was successfully transplanted from South Africa to Taiwan in the early 1950s. Cane yield of this Nico 310 is higher than the POJ varieties by some 10,000 kilograms of cane per hectare.[7]

Of equal importance to the varietal improvement in seeds to raise crop yield is the increased application of commercial fertilizers. In most instances, those improved and better seeds also consume more fertilizer. Rise in crop yield could not have been nearly as dramatic without increasing the application of commercial fertilizers. The Polai rice is again an illustrative example. This hybrid Polai rice is sensitive to soil fertility and moisture conditions; it also requires good farming techniques. The sharp decline in crop yield for Polai rice in 1945 shows dramatically how the character of high yield of the improved varieties of seeds depends on the adequate application of fertilizers. In 1945, when the supply of commercial fertilizers was extremely inadequate, yield for Polai rice fell greatly to 1,181 kilograms per hectare, which was considerably lower than the average yield of 1,320 kilograms per hectare for Chailai rice in the same year.[8] The amount of chemical fertilizers applied increased very rapidly throughout the entire period under consideration. Even though the consumption of commercial fertilizers per crop area was lower in 1956–1960 than in 1936–1940, consumption per unit of land area had increased from 0.564 metric ton in 1936–1940 to 0.758 metric ton in 1956–1960 (see Table 35). Yields per unit of crop area are highly correlated with the amount of chemical fertilizers applied per unit of crop area. The correlation coefficient is found to be as high as +0.979. In addition to the varietal improvement in seeds and the

7. Information contained in this section was provided by Mr. Tien-Tso Chang of Taiwan Sugar Corporation, Taiwan, to whom the writer is greatly indebted.
8. *Agricultural Statistics,* p. 20.

increased use of chemical fertilizers, improved cultural practices, greater and more efficient use of compost manure, reduced crop losses from insect pests and diseases through the use of pesticides and disease-resistant varieties of seeds and improved irrigation and drainage facilities have had a favorable effect in enhancing crop yield per unit of crop land during the period.[9]

TABLE 35

Consumption of Commercial Fertilizers
(Unit: Metric ton/hectare)

Period	Consumption per Crop Area	Consumption per Land Area
1901–1905	0.024	0.027
1906–1910	0.053	0.059
1911–1915	0.086	0.099
1916–1920	0.154	0.176
1921–1925	0.177	0.206
1926–1930	0.259	0.306
1931–1935	0.323	0.411
1936–1940	0.446	0.564
1941–1945	0.241	0.301
1946–1950	0.128	0.190
1951–1955	0.332	0.557
1956–1960	0.432	0.758

Source: See Tables 16, 17, and 21.

When the output of any period is divided into two parts—(1) the part which would have been obtained had yield per unit of crop area remained unchanged since the base period of 1901–1905, and (2) that part attributable to the net change in yield per unit of crop area from the base period crop yield—it is found that 34 percent of the increment in the output from 1901–1905 to 1936–1940 and 21 percent from 1901–1905 to 1956–1960 is attributed to rises in yield per unit of crop area.[10] There is, however, a notable difference between the growth experience

9. T. H. Shen, *Agricultural Planning and Production*, pp. 9–15.
10. For the method of estimation, see the note of Table 40, Part II. These are low estimates of the increment in output because of increases in yield per unit of crop area. A portion of the increment is attributable to the interaction of increases in yields and increases in crop area.

in the period of 1901 to 1940 and that of the period of 1946–1960. Whereas in the former period both crop area and yield per unit of crop area had shown comparable increases (85-percent enlargement in crop area and 78-percent rise in yield per unit of crop area), the latter period was characterized by further expansions in crop area by some 50 percent without any accompanying gains in yield per unit of crop area. This suggests that a greater intensified degree of land utilization enhanced farm output in the period of 1946–1960.

To a large extent, the existing techniques in agriculture determine the degree with which resources are utilized. Land, as a limitative factor, conditions possible maximum utilization of all other factors in agriculture. And the effect of the increased degree of utilization of other resources on farm output must be crystallized and shown as the effect of a more intensified rate of land utilization on farm output. Increased utilization rate may be taken as a first approximation to reduce the dimension of the problem of gauging the effect of the changes in the degree of resources utilization on the computed unexplained output.

The method and procedure employed here in deriving the aggregate input index make no allowance for the changes in the degree of intensity of land utilization. Physical land area is taken as input. Apparently, the aggregate input index reflects only movements along the extensive margins of land. Thus, if crop area, which measures both cultivated land area and the frequency of its utilization, is taken as land input to calculate the aggregate input index, the derived aggregate input index will contain both the changes in the extensive as well as intensive use of land. The difference between the two input indices will then represent the effect of changes in the intensity of land utilization. As defined in Chapter 6, I_t is the aggregate input index of year t in relation to year 0, and

$$I_t = {}_1X_t^a \cdot {}_2X_t^b \cdot {}_3X_t^c \cdot {}_4X_t^d$$

where ${}_1X_t$, ${}_2X_t$, ${}_3X_t$, and ${}_4X_t$ represent indices of land input, labor input, working capital, and fixed capital input, respectively. By the same procedure, let ${}_1X'_t$ = the index of crop area in year t:

$$I'_t = {}_1X'^a_t \cdot {}_2X_t^b \cdot {}_3X_t^c \cdot {}_4X_t^d$$

where I'_t stands for the aggregate input index of year t with land input measured in terms of crop area. And let G'_{ct} be the expected output index of year t. As shown in the previous chapter, in the absence of technical change,

$$G_{ct} = I_t$$

and $$y_{ct} = G_{ct} \cdot y_0$$

Similarly,

$$G'_{ct} = I'_t$$

and $$y'_{ct} = G'_{ct} \cdot y_0$$

Therefore, $$y'_{ct} - y_{ct} = (I'_t - I_t)y_0$$

where $y'_{ct} - y_{ct}$ measures the expected output attributed to the changes in the intensity of land utilization. As noted above, the changes in the rate of intensity of land utilization were probably the only case of intensification of resource use of any consequence. Accordingly, $y'_{ct} - y_{ct}$ can be regarded as the expected output attributed to changes in the degree of resource utilization. The result is presented in Table 36. For comparison purposes, the five-year averages for the unexplained output assignable to the changes in intensity of land utilization for the period of 1926–1960 are summarized in Table 37. As estimated here, 24.2 percent of the unexplained output in 1926–1930 is attributed to the changes in the degree of land utilization as compared with 20.0 percent for the period of 1956–1960. The highest is 61.0 percent for 1946–1950; the lowest amounts to 14.6 percent for 1936–1940.

Expansion in irrigation facilities can substantially raise the degree of intensity of land utilization. Non-irrigated land can be converted into double-cropping paddy field if irrigation water is made available and adequate.[11] The fact that most multiple-cropping practices are carried out on the paddy field attests to the importance of irrigation in increasing the degree of resource utilization. The rapid expansion in irrigation facilities is one of the outstanding features characterizing the development of agriculture for the period of 1901–1940 and especially between 1920 and 1940. That the Japanese developmental policy had empha-

11. The paddy field that can grow one rice crop each year is called a single-cropping paddy field; it is called a double-cropping paddy field if it can grow two rice crops a year.

TABLE 36

Residuals Attributed to Changes in the Degree of
Resource Utilization

Year	Aggregate Input [a] I'_t	Aggregate Input I_t	Increase in Output Attributed to Change in the Intensity of Land Use [b]
1903	100.0	100.0	0
1904	106.7	107.4	−13.7
1905	108.7	108.7	0
1906	112.7	112.4	7.8
1907	118.0	117.6	7.8
1908	130.6	128.9	33.3
1909	149.5	148.6	17.6
1910	155.5	156.0	−9.8
1911	156.4	155.0	27.4
1912	162.7	161.4	23.5
1913	155.8	153.7	41.2
1914	157.3	154.7	50.9
1915	167.4	165.2	43.1
1916	179.3	177.8	29.4
1917	185.1	183.5	31.4
1918	178.5	175.7	54.9
1919	182.8	180.1	52.9
1920	183.7	183.4	5.9
1921	182.7	182.0	13.7
1922	179.2	176.6	50.9
1923	184.5	182.3	43.1
1924	195.3	191.8	68.6
1925	203.1	199.0	80.3
1926	205.9	202.0	76.4
1927	209.1	205.5	70.5
1928	215.2	211.9	64.7
1929	212.6	209.8	54.9
1930	217.9	213.2	92.1
1931	225.0	218.9	119.5
1932	223.6	215.4	160.7
1933	232.8	224.4	164.6
1934	241.8	233.1	170.5
1935	253.8	242.9	213.6
1936	257.2	246.7	205.8
1937	258.4	249.6	172.4

TABLE 36 (Continued)

Year	Aggregate Input [a] I'_t	Aggregate Input I_t	Increase in Output Attributed to Change in the Intensity of Land Use [b]
1938	260.1	252.6	147.0
1939	264.6	255.4	180.3
1940	268.1	257.3	211.6
1941	260.2	249.0	219.5
1942	245.9	236.7	180.3
1943	242.8	234.6	160.7
1944	204.6	195.9	170.5
1945	138.4	139.6	−23.5
1946	159.7	157.5	43.1
1947	210.3	197.5	250.8
1948	228.4	210.7	346.8
1949	234.9	213.7	415.4
1950	264.1	238.7	497.7
1951	277.4	250.4	529.1
1952	294.3	265.1	572.2
1953	300.0	270.2	584.0
1954	312.7	281.0	621.2
1955	307.5	277.0	597.7
1956	315.3	282.6	640.8
1957	319.6	285.1	676.1
1958	323.6	288.3	691.7
1959	321.0	288.6	634.9
1960	331.9	294.3	736.8

a. Crop area is used as land input.
b. Computed from the form $(I'_t - I_t) \cdot y_o$, where y_o = NT\$1,959.6 million.
Source: See Table 17, Table 23, and the text of this chapter.

sized the provision of irrigation facilities is clearly shown from the magnitude of expansion in irrigated area and in paddy field during that period. Irrigated area increased from 150,456 hectares in 1903 to 545,092 hectares in 1942, an increase over 260 percent; [12] paddy field from 206,753 hectares in 1917 to 529,610 hectares in 1940, an increase

12. *Statistical Summary,* Table 214.

TABLE 37

*Percentage of the Residuals Assignable to Changes in the
Intensity of Land Utilization, 1926–1960*

Period	Residuals [a] (In millions of NT$)	Assigned (In millions of NT$)	Percent of Total
1926–1930	296.7	71.7	24.2
1931–1935	924.8	165.8	17.9
1936–1940	1,255.2	183.4	14.6
1941–1945	632.5	141.5	22.4
1946–1950	509.8	310.8	61.0
1951–1955	1,774.7	580.8	32.7
1956–1960	3,377.5	676.1	20.0

a. The unexplained output computed from the same base year, 1903.
Source: Computed from Tables 25 and 36.

of 150 percent.[13] Data on the detailed classifications of land are not
available before 1917, but between 1917 and 1940 double-cropping
paddy fields increased by 60 percent from 201,888 to 324,203 hectares,
and single-cropping paddy fields increased by some 73 percent from
118,640 to 205,407 hectares.[14] Again, the development experience in
the period of 1946–1960 is notably different from that of the period of
1901–1942. There has been virtually no further advancement in the
physical irrigation facilities in 1946–1960 in comparison with 1940.
Total irrigated area increased to 570,848 hectares in 1960, which is
merely 25,754 hectares above the level of 1942. While the double-cropping paddy field in 1960 was above the 1940 level by some 5,000 hectares, the single-cropping paddy field dropped by 6,880 hectares.[15] The
expansion in paddy fields during the period 1946–1960, as shown in
Table 38, reflects largely the result of reconstruction and repairing of
the irrigation system damaged during the years between 1943 and 1945.
Despite the fact that physical facilities of the irrigation system had
ceased to expand in the period of 1946–1960, greater efficiency in utilizing the established facilities was made possible through the so-called rotational system to distribute irrigation water.[16]

13. *Agricultural Statistics,* Table 1, Part II.
14. *Ibid.*
15. *Agricultural Yearbook,* 1961 edition, p. 20.
16. See Taiwan, Committee on the Promotion of Rotational Irrigation, *Rotational Irrigation.*

TABLE 38

Changes in Land Classifications, 1920–1960 [a]

(Unit: Hectare)

| Period | Total Arable Land | Paddy Field | | Dry Land |
		Double Cropping	Single Cropping	
1920	749,419	246,484	120,693	382,242
1921–1925	758,538	255,404	111,967	391,167
1926–1930	800,917	284,208	106,002	410,708
1931–1935	820,305	304,236	133,678	382,391
1936–1940	856,108	321,819	204,659	329,629
1941–1945	837,029	309,257	206,451	321,320
1946–1950	852,911	311,946	209,800	331,165
1951–1955	873,962	328,349	204,854	340,758
1956–1960	875,897	333,051	198,004	345,042

a. Each change can be determined by subtracting each total from that of the preceding period.
Source: Computed from data taken from *Agricultural Statistics*, p. 11, and *Agricultural Yearbook*, 1961 edition, p. 20.

The provision of irrigation was probably the crucial factor contributing to the rise in the multiple-cropping index and the expansion in crop area during the period of 1901–1943. The part of the computed unexplained output of the period which has been considered attributable to the factor of changes in the intensity of land utilization could probably be taken, for practical purposes, as a high estimate of the contribution of irrigation to farm output. This estimate may very likely be the maximum possible ceiling because better varieties of seeds, improved cultural practices, and greater use of fertilizers could also serve to shorten the growing period of crops to allow greater intensity of land use. In contrast with the growth experience in the prewar period, expansion in irrigation has little significance in raising the degree of intensity of land use. Whereas the crop area in the period of 1956–1960 was augmented by 50 percent and the multiple-cropping index raised by some 38 percent in comparison with 1936–1940, irrigation facilities in 1956–1960 remained at about the same level as in 1936–1940. A simple correlation analysis between the irrigated area (taken to be the independent variable) and multiple-cropping index gives the following result:

For 1903–1942: $Y = 100.74 + 0.0516X$
                   $S_{y.x} = 3.02$ $r = 0.8943$
For 1946–1960: $Y = 123.68 + 0.0808X$
                   $S_{y.x} = 49.3$ $r = 0.12$

The result confirms the above-expressed view that while expansion of irrigation was highly correlated with multiple-cropping index, i.e., the intensity of land utilization during the period from 1903 to 1942, the two had little connection in the latter period from 1946 to 1960.[17] This is of course not to imply that irrigation had lost its place in augmenting farm output during the latter period. Rather, the implication is that the increased intensity in land use in the latter period, when irrigation facilities remained at a standstill at the 1936–1940 level, must be explained by factors other than irrigation.

The availability of irrigation water can not only substantially raise the degree of land utilization through the conversion of non-irrigated dry

17. Data on irrigated area for 1901 and 1902 are not available.

land to paddy field and single-cropping paddy field to double-cropping field but can also improve land productivity. The improvement in land productivity brought about by irrigation water can be deemed a low estimate of the contribution of irrigation to farm output.[18] Following this line of reasoning, one can gauge the contribution of irrigation to farm output through changes in the productivity of land. Assuming that market prices of different types of land reflect their average productivities, the increased output attributed to the changes in land productivity can be estimated and identified according to the information on the changes in land classifications based on irrigation status as shown in Table 38. The estimate so obtained is presented in Table 39.

It appears that changes in land irrigation status account for as much as 38 percent of the increment of the unexplained output between 1921–1925 and 1926–1930, 30 percent of the increment between 1926–1930 and 1931–1935, and over 90 percent between 1931–1935 and 1936–1940; but for 1951–1955 and 1956–1960, these changes account for less than 0.01 percent of the increment of the unexplained output.[19] The statement here made is probably oversimplified. Irrigation and other technical changes in agriculture are highly complementary. Other technical changes probably also played a part in differentiating the productivity of lands with different irrigation status.

Reference has been made repeatedly to the distinctive experience in years between 1946 and 1960 in contrast with the growth pattern in the period of 1901–1942. In the latter period, whereas the degree of resource utilization had considerably increased, in terms of expansion in crop area and rise in multiple-cropping index, physical irrigation facilities remained at the same level as in 1936–1940. How was this achievement during the period realized? Here again, varietal improvement in seeds made the crucial contribution. The most outstanding case is the improved cane varieties Nico 310. These improved cane varieties are not only more productive in terms of cane yield per hectare and high sugar-

18. This estimate only takes account of the changes in land productivity attributed to the availability of irrigation water without considering the changes in land intensive margin.

19. The average of the unexplained output for 1921–1925 is −110.2 millions of New Taiwan Dollars; the average for 1926–1930 is NT$296.7 million. An increment status is 158.0 million or 38 percent of the increment of the unexplained output between two periods. Other figures are derived according to the same procedure.

TABLE 39

Estimates of Output Assigned to Changes in Land Irrigation Status

Period	Increment in Output [a]
1921–1925	16.9
1926–1930	158.0
1931–1935	179.6
1936–1940	313.5
1941–1945	−79.9
1946–1950	32.7
1951–1955	122.6
1956–1960	1.9

a. The method of estimation is as follows: (1) The average land value in 1960 was NT$111,084 per hectare: NT$152,042 per hectare for double-cropping paddy field, NT$100,792 per hectare for single-cropping paddy field, and NT$80,417 per hectare for dry land. If market prices of land with different irrigation status measure their productivities, productivity of double-cropping paddy field is 136.87 percent (NT$111,084 divided into NT$152,042) of the overall land productivity as shown in Table 32, 90.73 percent for a single-cropping paddy field, and 72.39 percent for dry land. Based on these ratios, it is easy to obtain land productivity according to irrigation status for different periods. (2) Multiplying the net changes in double-cropping paddy field and single-cropping paddy field with correspondent productivity, the sum is taken to be the increment of output attributed to changes in irrigation status; for 1931–1935 and 1936–1940, the sums are net of changes in dry land. In these two periods, total area of dry land declined as a result of expansion in irrigation. The contribution of irrigation to farm output apparently ought to be net of the output that would otherwise have been produced on dry land.

Source: Data on market prices of land in 1960 are taken from E. L. Rada and T. H. Lee, *Irrigation Investment in Taiwan: An Economic Analysis of Feasibility, Priority and Repayability Criteria*, Table 21, p. 48; data on land classification, see Table 38.

to-cane ratio than old POJ varieties, as already discussed above, but they are suitable for ratooning.[20] The nature of the improved varieties made possible shortening the average cane growing period from about 18 months to 12 months.[21] Polai rice is another illuminating case. The successful development of improved Polai varieties in the period required only a four-month growing period, which is shorter than the four-and-one-half month growing period of the native Chailai varieties. The shortened rice-growing period made possible the planting of a winter catch crop besides two crops of rice a year in the central part of Taiwan. In addition, this shorter growing period for rice also permitted sandwiching another summer crop between the first and second rice crop.[22] That makes a total of four crops in a year on a given piece of land in that region. In the southern part of Taiwan a three-crop system was hardly attainable because that region has a short rainy season. The replacement of the native Chailai varieties with the improved Polai varieties that have a shorter growing period insured a three-crop system in southern Taiwan.

The introduction of ingenious devices to the rotating system is another important factor that has served to lift the rate of intensity of land utilization. The improvement in the crop rotating system is best demonstrated by the introduction of the intercropping practices. It was found possible, for example, to plant a crop, such as tobacco, jute, sweet potatoes, or sugar cane, from 10 to 20 days before the harvest of the preceding paddy crop.[23] As a result, a three-crop system in a year is definitely assured. This intercropping system was found also feasible in cane fields and therefore was commonly practiced. Sweet potatoes, peanuts, soybeans, or rapeseed were interplanted with sugar cane.[24] Crop area can be then greatly increased without any noticeable adverse effect on cane growing.

Apparently, through these land-saving devices in combination with the varietal improvement of seeds, the rapid rise in multiple-cropping

20. The ratooning practice is to keep cane root intact and sprout sugar cane from the root in the succeeding season. This can considerably shorten the growing period of cane.

21. T. H. Shen, *Agricultural Planning*, p. 13.

22. *Ibid.,* p. 14.

23. *Ibid.,* p. 15.

24. *Ibid.*

index and crop area was made possible without any additional investment in irrigation. Even if there was little addition to the basic irrigation facilities in the period of 1946–1960, the existing establishment has been utilized more efficiently and more intensively through the rotating device to distribute irrigation water.

The increased farm output was realized in many, quite different ways over the long period of time. According to the input package applied, the whole period can be divided into three distinctive sub-periods at least, in spite of the fact that the exact date is somewhat arbitrary. In the first period, 1901 to 1920, the situation can be regarded as a movement toward Schultz's traditional agriculture. The increased farm output was realized almost solely through the increasing amount of traditional inputs applied in agriculture, especially the increased use of land service and fixed capital service. As additions of lesser quality were made to the acreage under cultivation, resource productivity declined in the first period. This period witnessed little change in the rate of resource utilization, as shown in the relatively unchanged index of multiple cropping, and little change in technology *per se* for yield per unit of crop area actually declined. The second period, 1920 to 1943, can be considered as a period of transition; the input mixture contains traditional as well as new inputs. Growth in farm output was brought about partially by the increased application of inputs of traditional type, such as extensive use of land, and partially by the introduction of new inputs into agriculture. Foremost among the latter were the application of chemical fertilizers, the expansion of irrigation system, and the introduction of improved seeds. Since both the extensive and intensive margins of land were exploited during this second sub-period, the index of multiple cropping showed a moderate increase from 110.72 in 1920 to 129.86 in 1940. Aggregate resource productivity was some 46 percent higher in 1936–1940 than in 1916–1920. And yield per unit of land area in 1936–1940 increased 100 percent when crop yield per unit of land area in 1901–1905 is used as the basis of comparison. The increased degree of land utilization in this period was primarily a result of the provision of irrigation, and technical change *per se* contributed to the raised yield per unit of crop area. In the third period, 1946 to 1960, the agricultural sector had been transformed into a modern and highly productive one. Traditional inputs lost their importance in furnishing additional

TABLE 40

PART I:

Increment in Output and the Explanatory Factors

(1903 = 100)

Period	Increment in Output [a]	Input Changes [b]	Residuals [c]	Changes in Land Intensity [d]	Land Improvement [e]
1906–1910	506.8	640.8	−134.0	11.3	—
1911–1915	697.7	1,137.0	−439.3	37.2	—
1916–1920	1,095.8	1,569.6	−473.8	34.9	—
1921–1925	1,581.7	1,691.9	−110.2	51.3	16.9
1926–1930	2,422.5	2,125.8	296.7	71.7	158.0
1931–1935	3,412.3	2,487.5	924.8	165.8	179.6
1936–1940	4,240.0	2,984.8	1,255.2	183.4	313.5
1941–1945	2,810.8	2,178.3	632.5	141.5	−79.9
1946–1950	2,558.4	2,030.6	509.8	310.8	32.7
1951–1955	5,081.3	3,306.6	1,774.5	580.8	122.6
1956–1960	7,057.2	3,679.7	3,377.5	676.1	1.9

a. The series is obtained by subtracting the total output of 1903 from the average output of each period. For output series see Table 3.

b. Subtract the output of the base year from the expected output of each period. The expected output series is taken from column 3, Table 25.

c. Unexplained output series is taken from column 4, Table 25.

d. Taken from Table 36.

e. Taken from Table 39. The increment in the residuals resulting from land improvement can be obtained by subtracting figures in column 4 from each preceding period.

Source: See Tables 3, 25, 36, 37, and 39.

TABLE 40
PART II:

Increment in Crop Output and the Explanatory Factors

(*1903 = 100*)

Period	Increment in Output [a]	Increase in Yield per Crop Area [b]	Increase in Crop Area [b]	Interactions [b]
1906–1910	446.0	25.6	414.0	6.4
1911–1915	589.5	−8.2	600.6	−2.9
1916–1920	915.7	145.3	708.5	61.9
1921–1925	1,331.0	325.6	834.7	170.7
1926–1930	2,057.8	644.5	1,018.9	394.5
1931–1935	2,935.1	917.8	1,300.4	716.9
1936–1940	3,672.3	1,307.2	1,428.9	1,034.2
1941–1945	2,634.1	751.5	1,297.1	585.5
1946–1950	2,477.5	263.6	1,911.1	302.7
1951–1955	4,298.6	718.8	2,500.1	1,079.7
1956–1960	5,732.4	1,159.0	2,696.1	1,877.3

a. Livestock and poultry products are not included.

b. The method of estimation is as follows: Let Y be average yield per crop area in the base year, C_0 crop area in the base period, Y_t average yield per crop area in year t, and C_t crop area in year t. Total output, exclusive of livestock and poultry products, in year t can be written as: $Q_t = Y_t (C_t)$
Similarly, $Q_0 = Y_0 (C_0)$
But, $Y_t = Y_0 + Y'$ and $C_t = C_0 + C'$: Y' and C' represent the increment in yield and in crop area, respectively. Therefore, $Q_t - Q_0 = C_0 Y' + Y_0 C' + C'Y'$
C_0Y' can be regarded as the increment in output attributed to increase in yield per unit of crop area, Y_0C' to increase in crop area, and $C'Y'$ to increase in yield per unit of crop area as well as increase in crop area. Apparently, the three individual components are additive.

Source: See Table 32.

sources of new income streams. Growth in farm output during the period was chiefly realized through the application of new inputs, the use of improved seeds characterized by high yield and a shorter growing period, and the introduction of land-saving devices to the crop rotating system. The outstanding experience in growth of farm output is the boosted degree of intensity rate of land use without new additions to the existing irrigation facilities. The productive nature of these new inputs in agriculture is clearly shown in the highest rate of productivity increase in this period in comparison with other sub-periods.

Table 40 summarizes the findings stated in this chapter.

Chapter 9

THE EFFECT OF RURAL EDUCATION AND RESEARCH ACTIVITIES ON FARM OUTPUT

In 1960 the total farm output of Taiwan was estimated as NT\$9,338 million valued at the 1952–1956 constant prices. The expected output of that year would be NT\$5,767.1 million based on the form: $I_t y_0$ (see equation 4, Chapter 7). Recall that I_t is the aggregate input index of the year t in relation to the year 0 and y_0 is the output in the year 0. The difference between the actual and the expected output of that year, which is some 38 percent of the actual output of 1960, represents the "unexplained" output of that year—unexplainable in terms of increases in conventional inputs. It is found that a portion of the "unexplained" output may be attributed to two concrete phenomena: the increased intensity of land utilization, in which irrigation played an important role, and the increased yields from each unit of crop area (see Chapter 8). But these two phenomena are only proximate causes of the growth in output. The underlying factors that have made increased yields and use of resources possible will be studied in this chapter. Although these improvements were in part a result of factors capable of treatment as conventional inputs—e.g., fertilizers as a current input and irrigation facilities as fixed capital or land improvement—a host of new, nontraditional inputs are required as co-operative agents within themselves as well as with the traditional inputs. Thus, irrigation requires new methods of cultivation, new farm enterprises, new seed varieties, improved fertilization, and other changes to produce anything like the maximum effect. In this chapter an attempt will be made to measure the contribution to farm output of these underlying factors: rural (formal) education and agricultural research, development, and extensions.

The way through which the farm output of Taiwan has increased suggests strongly the important place of rural education and agricultural research activities in Taiwan's agricultural development during the period under consideration. The increased farm output appeared to have been realized through the expansion of crop area—or, the degree of resource utilization—and improvement in crop yields per unit of crop area. Varietal improvement in seeds and greater application of fertilizers, among other things, are major factors that have made the great gains in crop yield possible. The development of better seeds characterized by a shorter growing period and improved crop rotational system served to raise the intensity of land utilization. The availability of those new, nonconventional inputs and the acquired skills of farm people in utilizing those modern farm inputs are therefore the principal sources of farm output growth. Although there is a body of knowledge that has been accumulated in advanced countries, these new, nonconventional inputs generally cannot be imported in any ready-made form. The character of high yield and/or a shorter growing period of new seed varieties, the method of fertilization, cultural practices, and method of irrigation are all pertinent to the particular conditions of an agriculture. Thus, these new and modern farm inputs can be made available only through research and development of the particular conditions. The development of new seed varieties, improved crop rotational system, better cultural practices, greater efficiency in utilizing irrigation water, and new methods of fertilization are all concrete results of research activities. In utilizing these new inputs, farm people are required to acquire new skills. For example, to adopt improved seeds, new methods of cultivation, fertilization, and irrigation are required. Extension services and formal education in rural areas are therefore important investment activities to equip farm people with the skills necessary to use these modern farm inputs.

The contribution of rural (formal) education to agricultural development in Taiwan probably did not take the form of producing highly trained agricultural scientists and technicians. There were as few as 200 students enrolled in agricultural colleges as late as 1940.[1] Agricultural scientists and technicians were predominantly Japanese nationals during the period of 1901–1944. In the postwar period, immigrated scientists and technicians from continental China dominated the agricultural scene. Although statistics show that the number of students enrolled in agricultural colleges and schools increased greatly during this period, graduates

1. *Statistical Summary,* p. 1227.

from agricultural colleges and schools either remained in cities or emigrated abroad. If there exists any difference in susceptibility and in ability to absorb new ideas and innovations between an uneducated person and one with a few years of schooling, the most plausible and conceivable way that formal education can contribute to farm output increases is that it transforms a person bound by tradition into one who is susceptible to change. From this point of view, the development of primary education probably had an important place in Taiwan's agricultural development. During the period of Japanese occupation, the emphasis of formal education was put on the expansion of primary education. The enrollment of students in primary schools increased very rapidly from 17,579 in 1901 to 670,000 in 1940.[2] The postwar period also witnessed a rapid expansion in primary education; attendance in those schools climbed from 850,097 in 1945 to 1,766,445 in 1960.[3] It is inconceivable that the rapid expansion of primary education during the period could have left agriculture unaffected.

In studying the effect of rural education and research activities on farm output in Japan's agriculture, Professor Tang argues that it is reasonable to assign most of the computed unexplained output to investment activities in the human agent, in view of the small impact of other factors upon farm output during the period of his study. He takes expenditures on rural education, agricultural research, development, and extensions as a single explanatory variable and proposes a distributed lag scheme to estimate the rate of return on those investments. The unexplained output is viewed as a function of the past investment activities in the human element. He derives a marginal efficiency of some 35 percent for those investment activities.[4]

Tang's distributed lag scheme contains an arithmetically rising phase followed by a geometrically converging phase. While this distributed lag scheme retains the apparent advantage of Koyck's simplified distributed lag form, it avoids the very restrictive time profile of immediate convergence implicit in Koyck's scheme. Reasoning that the effect of education will be gradually realized and will be continuously felt for an

2. *Ibid.*
3. *Statistical Abstract*, No. 15, Table 120; and *Statistical Book, 1962*, p. 137.
4. Anthony M. Tang, "Research and Education," pp. 27–41, 91–99.

unknown period after a maximum is reached, Tang asserts that the time shape assumed in his distributed scheme appeals both to intuition and logic. Specifically, his distributed lag takes the following form: [5]

$$y'_t = a \sum_{i=1}^{k} ih_{t-i} + ak \sum_{i=k+1}^{\infty} d^{i-k}h_{t-i} + u_t \quad (0 \le d < 1) \qquad (1)$$

From the difference between the following two equations:

$$y'_t = ah_{t-1} + 2ah_{t-2} + \cdots + kah_{t-k} + kadh_{t-k-1} + kad^2h_{t-k-2}$$
$$+ \cdots + u_t$$

$$dy'_{t-1} = adh_{t-2} + 2adh_{t-3} + \cdots + kadh_{t-k-1} + kad^2h_{t-k-2} + \cdots$$
$$+ du_{t-1}$$

he obtains

$$y'_t = a(1 - d) \sum_{i=1}^{k} ih_{t-i} + ad \sum_{i=1}^{k} h_{t-i} + dy'_{t-1} + u_t - du_{t-1} \quad (2)$$

This is the equation for fitting purposes; the parameters to be estimated are a, d, and k. The explanatory variable h in this case refers to investment outlays in rural education and agriculture research. The parameter k, denoting the year in which the time profile of the reaction coefficient reaches the peak, is treated by assigning successive values to it, beginning with $k = 1$. Parameters a and d are obtained by minimizing the sum of the squared residuals with respect to a and d and by solving the two derived equations. The a, d, and k values correspondent to the highest R^2 are then taken and used to estimate the long-run undiscounted social return to a money unit of outlays in research and education, given by the sums of the coefficients:

$$ak \left(\frac{k - 1}{2} + \frac{1}{1 - d} \right)$$

Autoregression of the disturbance terms in equation (1) leads to least-square bias.[6] Even if the disturbance terms, u_t, in equation (1) are

5. Tang, *ibid.*, p. 34.
6. L. M. Koyck, *Distributed Lags and Investment Analysis*, pp. 32–35.

assumed non-autoregressive, the composite disturbance terms in the derived equation (2) will be autocorrelated.[7] In order to overcome this difficulty, Tang follows Klein's thought by reversing the procedure and starting with an equation of the form: [8]

$$v_t = a(1 - d) \sum_{i=1}^{k} ih_{t-1} + ad \sum_{i=1}^{k} h_{t-i} + dy'_{t-1} + v_t \quad (0 \leq d < 1) \quad (3)$$

and derives from it a distributed lag scheme:

$$v'_t = a \sum_{i=1}^{k} ih_{t-i} + ak \sum_{i=k+1}^{t} d^{i-k}h_{t-i} + \sum_{i=1}^{t} d^{i-1}v_{t-i-1} + d^t y'_0 \quad (4)$$

Tang used equation (3) in the study of the effect of agricultural education and research investment on the computed unexplained output in Japanese agricultural development during 1880–1938. His findings, however, did not turn out quite as expected. The value of R^2 was generally low even at its maximum, and it had no central tendency; R^2 reached its maximum when k was 1 instead of in the neighborhood of 6 to 8 as expected. An immediate converging time profile seemed to give a better fit. He provides two explanations for that unexpected result: (1) the outmigration of farm youth to cities served as an offsetting factor, and (2) about one-tenth of the educational and research expenditures was allocated to plant and equipment whose influence upon the unexplained output is monotonically decreasing over time. For those two reasons the assumed arithmetically rising phase may be too drastic.

Nevertheless, the setting of Tang's study, Japan during 1880–1938, is undoubtedly much purer than the setting here. Tang faces an almost completely unchanged farm labor force, so he can justifiably disregard the effect of changes in qualitative attributes of labor force, such as sex and age composition, other than education. Also, the size of the agricultural sector, as indicated by labor, land, and number of farms, remained constant in Japan. But in the case of Taiwan, gainfully employed population increased from 922,000 in 1901 to 1,375,000 in 1960. Age composition of the gainfully employed population in agricul-

7. L. R. Klein, "The Estimation of Distributed Lags," *Econometrica*, XXVI (October 1958), p. 554.
8. Tang, *op. cit.*, p. 36.

ture could not have remained unchanged as the age composition of the total population had undergone significant change during the long-term period (see Table 15). Although known statistics suggest little change in the sex composition of the total population, female laborers in agriculture had definitely declined, as already noted above. More significant are the changes in the level of health as a result of the Japanese efforts in eradicating various diseases during the first two decades of the period, although the bearing of this improvement upon farm output is uncertain. One more significant aspect ought to be mentioned. When one faces an unchanged size of labor force, only the changes in the level of knowledge or skill are reflected in the data. That data reflect only changes in the level of stock of knowledge and/or skill is highly desirable because vertical expansion alone is concerned. The horizontal expansion of knowledge becomes important when the size of labor force has expanded, which is the case in Taiwan. Despite those complications, an attempt is made to gauge the contribution of agricultural research and education to farm output using Tang's distributed lag scheme.

Estimates are made based on three different distributed lag forms:

$$y'_t = a(1 - d) \sum_{i=1}^{k} i x_{t-i} + ad \sum_{i=1}^{k} x_{t-i} + dy'_{t-1} + v_t \tag{5}$$

$$y_t = ax_{t-1} + a(1 - d) \sum_{i=2}^{k} \frac{(1 + i)}{2} x_{t-i} + \frac{1}{2} ad \sum_{i=2}^{k} x_{t-i}$$
$$+ dy'_{t-1} + v_t \tag{6}$$

$$y'_t = ax_{t-1} + a(1 - d) \sum_{i=2}^{k} \frac{(4 + i)}{5} x_{t-i} + \frac{1}{5} ad \sum_{i=2}^{k} x_{t-i}$$
$$+ dy'_{t-1} + v_t \tag{7}$$

Equation (6) specifies a distributed lag scheme of the following form:

$$y'_t = a \sum_{i=1}^{k} \frac{1 + i}{2} x_{t-i} + a \frac{1 + k}{2} \sum_{i=k+1}^{\infty} d^{i-k} x_{t-i} + u_t \quad (0 \leq d \leq 1)$$

From the difference between the next two equations:

$$y'_t = ax_{t-1} + 1\frac{1}{2}ax_{t-2} + 2ax_{t-3} + \cdots + \frac{k+1}{2}ax_{t-k}$$

$$+ \frac{k+1}{2}adx_{t-k-1} + \frac{k+1}{2}ad^2x_{t-k-2}\ldots + u_t$$

$$dy'_{t-1} = adx_{t-2} + 1\frac{1}{2}adx_{t-3} + 2adx_{t-4} + \cdots + \frac{k+1}{2}adx_{t-k-1}$$

$$+ \frac{k+1}{2}ad^2x_{t-k-2} + \cdots + du_{t-1}$$

one obtains

$$y'_t = a\sum_{i=1}^{k}\frac{1+i}{2}x_{t-i} - ad\sum_{i=2}^{k}\frac{1+i}{2}x_{t-i} + \frac{1}{2}ad\sum_{i=2}^{k}x_{t-i}$$

$$+ dy'_{t-1} + u_t - du_{t-1}$$

or,

$$y'_t = ax_{t-1} + a(1-d)\sum_{i=2}^{k}\frac{1+i}{2}x_{t-i} + \frac{1}{2}ad\sum_{i=2}^{k}x_{t-i}$$

$$+ dy'_{t-1} + v_t$$

Equation (7) can be derived by the same procedure.

Equation (5) is Tang's equation (8); equations (6) and (7) are variations of equation (5) taking gradual arithmetically increasing phase. The computed unexplained output is y'_t, x_t is the explanatory variable consisting of rural education and research expenditures (see Table 41), and v_t is the disturbance term taken to be non-autocorrelated. If those random disturbance terms are disregarded, equations (5), (6), and (7) define the computed unexplained output as a function of the past investment in agricultural education and research.

Parameters to be estimated are a, d, and k. The method of estimating is the same as Tang's; that is, k is assigned successive values beginning with $k = 1$, and a and d are obtained by minimizing the sum of the squared residuals with respect to a and d and solving the two derived equations. All variables are expressed as deviations from their respective means to remove the constant terms as in equations (5), (6), and (7). The value of R^2 is then calculated for each set of a, d, and k values.

TABLE 41

Rural Education, Research Outlays, and "Unexplained" Output

Year	"Unexplained" Output (In millions of NT$)	Outlays on Rural Education and Research (In millions of NT$)	Deflator (1952–1956 = 100)
1903	0	11.6	2.26
1904	89.0	13.2	1.84
1905	188.2	13.5	2.16
1906	28.7	14.7	2.31
1907	119.4	15.6	2.85
1908	21.8	20.0	2.42
1909	−316.2	22.6	2.42
1910	−523.7	24.8	2.75
1911	−361.2	25.3	3.24
1912	−756.8	23.4	4.89
1913	−272.7	27.4	4.05
1914	−408.6	33.4	2.93
1915	−396.8	37.6	2.62
1916	−502.8	42.3	2.92
1917	−351.7	38.4	3.89
1918	−379.7	39.4	5.51
1919	−425.2	39.6	7.11
1920	−710.3	48.5	6.78
1921	−534.4	137.2	5.94
1922	−63.8	165.9	4.93
1923	−268.2	154.6	5.26
1924	118.9	137.2	5.93
1925	196.4	120.9	6.87
1926	61.7	132.2	6.62
1927	218.6	152.8	5.82
1928	276.0	161.1	6.04
1929	339.2	177.7	6.20
1930	588.1	224.0	4.97
1931	583.8	281.3	3.92
1932	1,365.1	232.2	4.59
1933	633.7	258.3	4.29
1934	916.5	236.1	4.87
1935	1,124.7	217.8	5.62
1936	1,279.9	238.5	5.82
1937	1,308.3	272.9	5.95
1938	1,539.3	274.8	6.52
1939	1,548.9	237.9	7.76
1940	599.4	272.0	8.69

TABLE 41 (Continued)

Year	"Unexplained" Output (In millions of NT$)	Outlays on Rural Education and Research (In millions of NT$)	Deflator (1952–1956 = 100)
1941	684.4	302.2	9.09
1942	1,001.1	332.7	10.01
1943	788.7	405.1	10.01
1944	702.1	313.9	14.07
1945	−13.8	90.0	23.96
1946	40.7	15.0	1,120.41
1947	−103.1	30.9	3,228.97
1948	349.5	36.4	24,470.58
1949	1,034.0	54.3	26.23
1950	1,227.9	119.2	42.30
1951	1,178.8	97.7	56.00
1952	1,454.6	78.6	79.28
1953	2,185.2	76.2	105.35
1954	2,002.2	122.2	89.33
1955	2,052.7	103.5	114.84
1956	2,606.6	324.1	117.54
1957	3,280.4	375.7	127.19
1958	3,752.8	364.9	132.73
1959	3,675.8	388.0	152.15
1960	3,571.8	349.0	197.45

Source: (1) Unexplained output series taken from Table 25. (2) Research and educational outlays for the period 1903–1944 are taken from *Statistical Summary*, Tables 348 and 366; for 1946–1950 data are taken from *Statistical Abstract*, No. 15, Table 52; the 1945 figure is a crude estimate based on data provided in Hsieh, *Taiwan Ten-Year*. Education outlays recorded are total educational outlays, expenditures on rural education is estimated by multiplying the ratio of agricultural population to total population. The allocation of research expenditures to agricultural research is estimated on the basis of the size of personnel in agricultural research institutes compared with other research institutes. (3) The deflator used here is the implicit price index obtained by dividing the output series, valued at 1952–1956 farm prices, into the current output series. Current output series compiled consists of 74 crops and products correspondent to the output series in 1952–1956 constant prices. Therefore, the implicit price index takes 1952–1956 as its base. Output series in current prices is compiled based on the data drawn from *Statistical Summary*, Tables 203, 204, 205, 206, 207, and 208 and Taiwan Provincial Food Bureau, *Taiwan Food Statistics Book*, Tables 7–12 for the period 1903–1944, taken from *Agricultural Yearbook*, 1961 edition, and *Statistical Abstract*, No. 15.

The unexplained output, taken here as the dependent variable, is the difference between the observed output and the expected output. The procedure of deriving the observed output has been described in Chapter 2. No repetition will be made here. Recall that the expected output is obtained by taking the aggregate input multiplied by farm output of the base year 1903. The aggregate input index contains four individual components: physical land area, labor, working capital, and fixed capital. Expenditures on rural education and agricultural research and development are taken here as the explanatory variable. Educational and research outlays are budgetary figures for the whole island. Rural education outlays are estimated and obtained by multiplying the total educational outlays by the ratio of agricultural population to total population for each year. Allocation of research outlays to agriculture is made according to the ratio of agricultural personnel in research institutes to the total number of personnel in research institutes. All outlays are originally recorded in terms of Old Taiwan dollars for the period of 1903–1948 and in New Taiwan dollars for 1949–1960. The outlays series is then deflated by the implicit price index, which is derived by dividing the output series in the 1952–1956 constant prices used for this study into the output series in current prices.

The results are shown in Table 42.

TABLE 42

Coefficients of a Lag Distribution Relating
the "Unexplained" Output to Agricultural
Education and Research Outlays

Equation 5, Set 1

k	R^2	a	d
1	0.9019	−0.1737	1.0245
2	0.9067	−0.3158	1.0528
3	0.9062	−0.2930	1.0611
4	0.9077	−0.2473	1.0578
5	0.9104	−0.1894	1.0511
6	0.9130	−0.1628	1.0475
7	0.9168	−0.1642	1.0458
8	0.9199	−0.1552	1.0421
9	0.9196	−0.1417	1.0420
10	0.9293	−0.1491	1.0395

TABLE 42 (Continued)

Equation 6, Set 2

k	R^2	a	d
2	0.9005	−0.3293	1.0438
3	0.9025	−0.3587	1.0520
4	0.9025	−0.3458	1.0520
5	0.9045	−0.3007	1.0494
6	0.9071	−0.2801	1.0478
7	0.9108	−0.2896	1.0467
8	0.9132	−0.2879	1.0440
9	0.9146	−0.2709	1.0451
10	0.9243	−0.2962	1.0440

Equation 7, Set 3

k	R^2	a	d
2	0.8946	−0.3072	1.0384
3	0.8878	−0.4669	1.0554
4	0.8818	−0.6027	1.0668
5	0.8832	−0.5926	1.0647
6	0.8826	−0.5698	1.0589
7	0.8817	−0.5846	1.0527
8	0.8808	−0.5620	1.0447
9	0.8786	−0.4996	1.0391
10	0.8773	−0.5029	1.0299

As shown in Table 42, the estimated values of *a* in all three distributed lag schemes are negative, and all *d* values are greater than one. The *d* value must be smaller than one if the fitting equations (5), (6), and (7) are to be derived from the difference between the two expanded forms defined in the assumed distributed lag scheme.[9] The unexpected and inconsistent result is no doubt caused by the nonhomogeneity of the time sample used. The nonhomogeneous character of the time sample covering the entire period has been clear from the earlier discussions. Moreover, the presence of the negative unexplained output during the first subperiod has likely affected the estimated coefficients. Also, it makes little sense to estimate the contribution of the nonconventional inputs to the unexplained output when the latter is negative. Presuma-

9. Please refer to equations (5), (6), and (7) and the lag distributed schemes they assume.

bly, the deterioration in the quality of the conventional inputs, as the expansion along the extensive margins takes on increasingly inferior quality of land, may have caused the unexplained output to be negative.

TABLE 43

Observed, Expected, and "Unexplained" Output, 1920–1940

(Unit: NT$1,000,000)

Year	Aggregate Input Index	Observed Output	Expected Output [a]	Unexplained Output
1920	100.0	2,883.6	2,883.6	0
1921	99.4	3,032.1	2,866.3	165.8
1922	97.6	3,396.8	2,814.4	582.4
1923	100.4	3,304.2	2,895.1	409.1
1924	106.3	3,877.4	3,065.3	812.1
1925	110.6	4,096.0	3,189.3	906.7
1926	112.1	4,020.1	3,232.5	787.6
1927	113.8	4,245.6	3,281.5	964.1
1928	117.1	4,428.4	3,376.7	1,051.7
1929	115.7	4,450.4	3,336.3	1,114.1
1930	118.6	4,766.0	3,419.9	1,346.1
1931	122.5	4,873.4	3,532.4	1,341.0
1932	121.7	5,486.1	3,509.3	2,076.8
1933	126.7	5,031.0	3,653.5	1,377.5
1934	131.6	5,484.3	3,794.8	1,689.5
1935	138.2	5,884.6	3,985.1	1,899.5
1936	140.0	6,114.2	4,037.0	2,077.2
1937	140.7	6,199.5	4,057.2	2,142.3
1938	141.6	6,489.2	4,083.2	2,406.0
1939	144.0	6,553.7	4,152.4	2,401.3
1940	145.9	5,641.4	4,207.2	1,434.2

a. $y_0 = $ NT$2,883.6
Source: See Tables 25 and 36.

For these reasons, an estimate of the coefficients a and d, based again on equations (5), (6), and (7), is made using only the sample data of the second subperiod between 1920 and 1940. However, the unexplained output series and the aggregate input index containing crop area, labor, working capital, and fixed capital input are independently computed with 1920 taken as the base year (see Table 43). The provision of irrigation, as already stated above, played an important part in raising the rate of intensity of land utilization during this second subperiod. To take crop area instead of land area as land input in constructing the aggregate input index is hopefully to obtain a residual series which would reflect technical change *per se*. As the sample used here covers a homogeneous time period, the estimated coefficients *a* and *d* are well behaved in all three distributed lag forms, as shown in Table 44. Taking the coefficients *a* and *d* corresponding to the highest R^2 value, when $k = 2$, and regarding the sum of the coefficients as the long-run undiscounted return from a unit of investment in rural education and research, one finds that investment of NT$1.0 led to a long-run social return of NT$7.83 to farm output during the period of 1920 to 1940. A marginal efficiency of some 180 percent is implied. However, Tang points out, ". . . insofar as only a portion of the investment was retailed in agriculture because of migration losses, it would be less than accurate to look upon this figure as a productivity statement." [10] Imposed on *a priori* ground, a more reasonable marginal efficiency of 55 percent, the rate of discount which equates the sum of the coefficients of NT$13.93 in Set 3 of Table 44 when $k = 6$ to NT$1.0, can be considered as the long-run social return to education and research in agriculture. [11]

Further, when $k = 6$, the time profile of the reaction coefficients is approximately what would be expected had the entire investment remained in agriculture. [12] Therefore, the estimate may be a low one because of migration losses. The reaction coefficients would have been higher had the investment remained in agriculture. On the other hand, one should take into account the offsetting consideration that other productivity-increasing factors that had been operative are not included in the explanatory variable *x*.

10. Tang, *op. cit.*, p. 97.
11. When $k = 6$, the time profile of the reaction coefficients is approximately what would be expected had the entire investment remained in agriculture; see Tang, *ibid*. The above estimate, however, may be regarded as low (subject to the offsetting consideration that in Taiwan's agriculture other productivity-increasing factors not accounted for by the explanatory variable *x* had been operative) because the reaction coefficients would have been higher had the entire investment remained in agriculture.
12. Tang, *ibid*.

TABLE 44

*Estimated Coefficients of Income Flows
from Investment in Agricultural Education
and Research*

Equation 5, Set 1

k	a	d	R^2
1	6.3210	0.3446	0.6576
2	1.5172	0.5201	0.7300
3	0.4712	0.6381	0.6663
4	0.4008	0.5344	0.6417
5	0.2932	0.5256	0.6015
6	0.1468	0.5707	0.5403
7	0.0689	0.5548	0.4732
8	0.0424	0.5170	0.3827

Equation 6, Set 2

k	a	d	R^2
2	1.7838	0.5455	0.6351
3	0.7285	0.6439	0.6781
4	0.6465	0.5394	0.6562
5	0.4571	0.5447	0.6087
6	0.2475	0.5776	0.5465
7	0.1199	0.5580	0.4758
8	0.0682	0.5246	0.3827

Equation 7, Set 3

k	a	d	R^2
2	2.3495	0.5232	0.6549
3	1.2276	0.6107	0.7036
4	1.0546	0.5067	0.6808
5	0.8001	0.5076	0.6344
6	0.4961	0.5423	0.5694
7	0.2700	0.5305	0.4908
8	0.1633	0.5043	0.3931

Chapter 10

SUMMARY AND CONCLUSIONS

According to the gross output index as compiled in this study, farm output of Taiwan increased 6.2 times in the years between 1901 and 1960. When farm output growth was measured in terms of average growth rate (compound) over the whole period, the increase in farm output was 3.14 percent per year. The average annual growth rate for the prewar years between 1901 and 1944 was 2.6 percent and, 8.57 percent for years between 1945 and 1960. However, the choice of period for the purpose of comparing rate of growth is significant since Taiwan's agricultural production throughout the period was subject to irregular short-term fluctuations. When the trend values are taken to abstract from these fluctuations, the average growth rate of 2.57 percent attained in the period of 1905–1940 can be reasonably regarded as the normal growth rate for the whole prewar period, and the average rate of 3.22 percent per year for the period of 1953–1960 seems to be representative of the normal pace of changes in farm output in the postwar period. Although changes in the productive capacity cannot be measured and cannot be inferred from changes in the growth rates, which are based on changes in actual production, the gross farm output index probably indicates the direction of capacity changes underlying Taiwan's agriculture. Changes in the composition of farm output in association with the growth in agricultural output fit well into the pattern generally assumed and accepted. Farm products with high income elasticities, such as fruits, vegetables, livestock, and poultry products, have gained in relative importance. The composition of farm output and therefore any change incurred probably have been influenced by the rapid population increase in the period. The relative decline of the share of special crops, largely cash crops, in the output total reflected the mounting demand for food crops as a result of rapid growth in population. The sharp fall in the relative share of sugar cane during the period of 1946–1960 is a case in point. Rice and sugar cane, the two major crops of Taiwan, have been continuously competing for the use of land throughout the period. In the prewar period, with the encouragement of the Japanese authority through subsidies and priority in acquiring commercial fertilizers and irrigation water, the area planted in sugar cane once reached 169,000 hectares, but land area for growing sugar cane has never been above 113,000 hectares in the postwar years. Increases in demand for food has forced the farm output composition to shift in favor of food crops.

The increased agricultural output was brought about in part by the increased farm inputs and in part by technological advancement broadly defined. In terms of gainfully occupied population in agriculture, labor input was augmented about 50 percent during the period under review. The rate of agricultural employment growth, however, was slower than the rate of growth of total population. This is attributed to two factors: (1) the size of labor force declined relative to the total population, and (2) the rate of labor participation in agriculture also declined both for male and female laborers. Enlargement of cultivated land area played an important part in raising farm output for the period of 1901–1920. But expansion in physical land area has ceased to be a contributing factor of the increment in agricultural output since 1940. Physical land area remained virtually unchanged between 1940 and 1960. A significant change in land utilization, from horizontal expansion to vertical expansion, had taken place at the time when the extensive margin of land cultivation had reached its limit. If changes in the irrigation status of land and changes in area of paddy field are indications, the quality of land has greatly improved. Whereas the area of irrigated land increased about 100 percent, the share of paddy field in the land total has gained 20 percent. The intensified rate of land utilization is shown in the remarkable rise in crop area and in the index of multiple cropping. Crop area has expanded from 505,000 hectares in 1901 to 1,117,000 hectares in 1940 and to 1,557,000 hectares in 1960; the index of multiple cropping has climbed from 109.8 in 1905 to 129.9 in 1940 and to 179.2 in 1960. Because of the narrow coverage, as represented by animal energy available in agriculture, the fixed capital series as estimated here has shown an improbable trend. The decline in the draft cattle population, which was the consequence of the development of modern transportation facilities in rural areas, is primarily responsible for the downward trend. The population of water buffalo, which is the principal source of animal energy in Taiwan's agriculture, has been relatively stable throughout the period. The most striking and significant change in farm input during the period is the rapid rise in the consumption of commercial fertilizers. Total consumption of commercial fertilizers per year has increased by some 47.5 times between 1901 and 1960. Consumption of chemical fertilizers per hectare (land area) has risen from 0.027 metric ton in 1901–1905 to 0.758 metric ton in 1956–1960. Because of the growth in human as well as animal population, the supply of farm-produced fertilizers must also have increased. Although their importance cannot be quantified, greater and more efficient application of farm-produced fertilizers probably played a part in raising farm output during the period.

Aggregate input, which contains land area, labor, working capital, and fixed capital, as estimated for this study, increased at an average rate of 2.0 percent (compound) per year. In the absence of technical change, increase in output was also expected to be at an average rate of 2.0 percent per year. With the particular method employed and assumptions made, the aggregate input index also defines changes in output in the absence of technical change. The observed farm output has, however, grown at a rate of 3.14 percent a year. The discrepancy of 1.14 percent between the observed and the expected growth rate of farm output is measured as the average rate of technical progress broadly defined, or the rate of technical change averaged about 1.14 percent (compound) per year. Of the 2.0 percent expected annual growth in farm output, 0.34 percent is attributed to increment in physical land area, 0.27 percent to labor, 1.27 percent to working capital input, and 0.11 percent to fixed capital input. A high rate of 3.2 percent of technical change was attained in the period of 1946–1960; the next highest rate was 2.9 percent in 1921–1930. The presence of the disparity between increment in input and increment in output implies changes in factor productivity. Productivity of land has risen by 180 percent, labor by 230 percent, and fixed capital input by 215 percent. Productivity of aggregate input has increased by 60 percent. Improvement in resource productivity was mainly made in the two periods of 1926–1940 and 1951–1960.

Together with the remarkable growth in farm output, the period of 1901–1960 shows marked improvement in transportation facilities, public health conditions, and general socio-economic frameworks. All of these have served to increase the output, even though their quantitative importance cannot be assessed statistically. A portion of the increment in farm output is attributed to two concrete phenomena: increases in the degree of utilization of land and in the yield from each unit of crop area. Varietal improvement in seeds and greater application of fertilizers, among other things, are the two most important factors underlying the gains in yield per unit of crop area. The introduction of better seed varieties characterized by a shorter growing period, changed cultural practices, and improved crop rotation also served to raise the intensity of land use. The provision of irrigation, too, played an important part in this connection. According to the estimates made in this study, 15 to 30 percent of the computed unexplained output can be attributed to the factor of changes in resource utilization. Yields per unit of crop area have risen by 80 percent when the period is taken as a whole. Of the five major crops of Taiwan—rice, sugar cane, sweet potatoes, peanuts, and tea—all but tea have gained substantially in yield from each unit of crop area. Yield of sugar cane from each unit of crop area rose by 160 percent, that of sweet potatoes by 95 percent, that of rice by 87 percent, and that of peanuts by 75 percent.

The supply of the modern, nontraditional farm inputs and the acquired skills of farm people in utilizing them constitute the major sources of growth of agricultural output. However, they are the proximate causes of output growth. The development of new seed varieties, new cultural practices, new methods of irrigation and fertilization, and the improvement in crop rotation are all concrete results of research activities. And they are made available through investment in agricultural research. The skills of farm people to utilize effectively new inputs can be acquired through investment in farm people. Thus, agricultural research and rural education are the principal underlying factors.

In view of the input package used, the period under consideration can be divided into three distinctive subperiods. The development of agriculture in the first twenty years was characterized by the employment of traditional types of input alone. The input package of agriculture in the next twenty years contained both traditional and nontraditional inputs. Increases in farm output in the years between 1946 and 1960 resulted primarily from a reliance on new, nontraditional farm inputs. Rise in resource productivity took place in the second and third subperiods.

This fact confirms Schultz's view that the supply of nontraditional inputs holds the key to growth agriculture. For when the extensive margins of land and the profitability of investing in other traditional inputs were exhausted, the growth process would have halted probably during the second subperiod had the infusion of new inputs not taken place. The growth experience in the prewar period is significantly different from that of the postwar years. Whereas in the prewar period increases in farm output can be attributed mainly to the improvement in yield per unit of crop area, the increased output in the postwar period has been realized through changes in the degree of resource utilization, more specifically, that of land. In addition, whereas the provision of irrigation played an important role in the moderate rise of resource utilization in the prewar period, the increased rate of intensity of land utilization in the postwar years was achieved without additions to the basic facilities of irrigation. Increased utilization of land in the postwar years was made possible through new seed varieties with shorter growing periods and an improved rotational irrigation system.

The most significant and distinctive fact of Taiwan's experience in developing its agriculture is that all these remarkable achievements were accomplished without changing the small farm-holding system. Average farm size throughout the period has never been larger than 2.0 hectares per farm household. The fact that the highest rate of technical progress of 3.2 percent per year was attained in the period 1951–1960—a period in which average farm size fell to 1.2 hectares—suggests the insignificance of economies of farm scale. Statistics of farm size distribution indicate that there was no significant land consolidation movement taking place during the period. Farms of a size under 2.0 chias—equivalent to 1.94 hectares—dominated the scene throughout the period.

The pattern of Taiwan's agricultural development underscores the important place of investment in the human agent in economic growth. The growth experience in Taiwan's agricultural development also supports the view that the rate of return on such investment is high. An investment of NT$1.0 in agricultural research and rural education could contribute, according to the estimates made in the study, as much as NT$13.93 to gross farm output in the long run. The long-run social return to education and research in agriculture is estimated to have a marginal efficiency as high as 55 percent. According to Tang's study, the long-run social return to those investment activities in Japan produced a marginal efficiency of some 35 percent.[1] The two estimates should not be taken without reservations, but the fact that a high social return to investment in the human agent has been realized both in the Japanese and Taiwan's experiences in developing their agricultures remains to be proved otherwise.

The experience of Taiwan in developing its agriculture has the following outstanding qualities: (1) innovations in agriculture emphasized the use of the limitative and untransferable factor of land and the abundant factor of labor in agriculture, (2) technical innovations used were compatible with the existing small farm-holding system so that a technical revolution in agriculture was accomplished without a parallel social revolution of a large-scale land consolidation movement in agriculture, (3) since all technical innovations stressed the use of abundant and untransferable factors with little opportunity cost, they demanded few scarce factors of the economy, (4) capital outlays needed to carry out these new innovations were small and, in addition, could be drawn from the agricultural sector itself, and (5) institutional frameworks constituted an important input in augmenting farm output.

In comparison with the Japanese experience in agricultural development, the growth experience of Taiwan offers few new methods that are unknown or unused in Japan. In many important aspects, the two cases are strikingly similar. As in Taiwan, the Japanese agricultural development encompasses two important forms of improvements: [2] (1) land improvement in which the provision of irrigation and drainage facilities and the reclamation of some arable land had been important, and (2) improvements in seed varieties, methods of cultivation, and increased use of fertilizers. The high rate of growth in agriculture during the initial stage of Japanese industrialization has been viewed as a revolutionary process in comparison with the fastest growth rates of agricultural output in Europe.[3] The rate of Taiwan's agricultural development during the period from 1901 to 1960 seems to be even faster than the rate of growth in Japan's agriculture during the period from 1878 to 1917. In terms of gross farm output, the rate of growth of Taiwan's

1. Tang, "Research and Education," p. 97.
2. Gerald M. Meier, *Leading Issues in Development Economics,* p. 308.
3. *Ibid.,* p. 314.

agriculture during the period of 1901–1960 averaged 3.14 percent annually, compared with the 2.3-percent annual growth of new farm output in Japan for the period 1878 to 1917.[4] There are other evidences supporting the assertion that the achievement in Taiwan is more impressive than that of Japan. For example, whereas yield of rice per hectare during the 1878–1917 period increased 50 percent in Japan, yield of rice per hectare during the forty-year span between 1901 and 1940 in Taiwan rose by 54 percent. Land productivity in Japan improved by 80 percent between 1878 and 1917; it increased by 97 percent in Taiwan.[5] In spite of the fact that international comparisons are often misleading and that the comparison made here is not in strictly comparable terms, the speedy rate of Taiwan's agricultural development during the period is at least comparable to the growth rate of Japan's agriculture during the period between the Meiji Restoration and World War I.

The experience of Taiwan's achievement in the development of agricultural productivity has much to offer to other countries in the process of development. As revealed in the analysis of this study, the growth pattern of Taiwan's agriculture during the period under review stands as an additional historical example beside the Japanese experience to support the view that an agriculture of low-productivity can be transformed into a productive one through land-saving and land-intensive devices without drawing on scarce resources of an economy. Moreover, such agricultural improvement can be made under small holdings. Consolidation of small farming units into large farm units is not the necessary precondition that some economists have insisted upon in transforming a traditional and inefficient agriculture into a modern and efficient one. While a wholesale mechanization of agriculture could be a forceful way to break the vicious circle of poverty observed in underdeveloped countries, such a bold scheme requires not only heavy investment in agriculture and in industry but a socially revolutionary, large-scale land consol-

---

4. The Japanese rate of growth in agriculture is cited in Meier, *ibid.,* p. 304; the comparable rate of growth of agriculture for the period of 1901–1940 is 3.44 percent in Taiwan. The Japanese rate of growth in terms of gross farm output was somewhat higher than 2.3 percent. See Kazushi Ohkawa and others, *The Growth Rate of the Japanese Economy Since 1878.*

5. Meier, *op. cit.,* p. 36. Land and labor productivity is computed on the basis of net farm output.

idation movement in agriculture. In view of the resources required, this scheme is perhaps not a practical one for most countries labeled as underdeveloped. The experience of Taiwan is indicative of a feasible and practical alternative to contemporary underdeveloped countries in formulating their policy for developing their agriculture. A technical revolution compatible with the existing institutional arrangements in agriculture can be a principal source of economic growth. The key to the successful transformation of Taiwan's agriculture is the supply of new, nontraditional farm inputs and the acquired skills of farm people in utilizing them. The speedy rate of growth of Taiwan's agricultural output strongly indicates that there are plenty of latent, rewarding opportunities in a traditional agriculture that can be tapped quickly by making those nontraditional inputs available. The availability of new, nontraditional farm inputs and the acquisition of skills of farm people require investment in agricultural research and education. Therefore, the growth experience of Taiwan underlines the importance of investment activities in the human agent. It also shows how much can be accomplished in developing agriculture by concentrating efforts on agricultural research and education. Although contemporary developing nations, as newcomers, have the advantage of drawing freely from accumulated knowledge, the supply of new farm inputs and required skills can be made available only through investing in research and education.

Economists have long recognized the importance of the so-called social overhead investment to general economic development. The experience of Taiwan in developing its agriculture also suggests that a minimum level of social overhead investment is necessary before direct improvement programs can be effectively implemented. Irrigation is one of the most important forms of social overhead investment in agriculture. The important place of irrigation in the growth of agriculture of Taiwan and Japan can hardly be exaggerated. Even though in the postwar period the degree of land utilization in Taiwan has been raised without additions to irrigation facilities, a well-established irrigation system had already been built. Education is another important aspect of social overhead capital. That economists have gradually come to re-emphasize the role of education in economic growth and to attempt to measure its contributions is a contemporary development. But merely to stress the role of education in economic progress is far too vague. The contribution of education to Taiwan's agricultural development did not take the form of producing agricultural scientists and technicians. It often happens in underdeveloped nations that returns on investment in higher education cannot be captured and capitalized in agriculture. But in comparison with return to investment in higher education, a greater portion of social return on investment in primary education in rural areas probably will be retained in the agricultural sector.

Finally, an important implication can be drawn from this study. There is evidence that economic development can proceed more smoothly if industrial and agricultural developments take place simultaneously. The supply of commercial fertilizers is a case in point. The importance of the role played by commercial fertilizers in Taiwan's agricultural development and in Japan as well needs no repetition here. It is very conceivable that the rate of farm output growth could probably be accelerated if an adequate supply of commercial fertilizers could be insured through the establishment of a domestic fertilizer industry. This is just one of many plausible ways that agricultural and industrial developments can be co-ordinated and integrated. It is true that industrial and agricultural developments in many aspects are competitive in demanding resources of a poor economy, but there is an indication that perhaps the competitive side of the matter has been overemphasized, and for that matter, the complementary character has been overlooked. If agricultural improvement can be accomplished without demanding scarce resources of an economy, as was the case in Taiwan's successful experience, the complementary side of industrial and agricultural development outweighs the competitive character of a concurrent development of agriculture and industry, and the substance of the matter becomes indisputable. To attain the highest possible overall rate of growth through optimum allocation of resources between industry and agriculture is not only economically desirable but feasible.

ESTIMATES OF GROSS OUTPUT AND INTER-MEDIATE PRODUCTS SERIES

Estimates of gross output from gross production data

Gross output, as defined in this study, is gross production after deducting seeds and feeds. In *Taiwan Food Balances: 1935–54* Ralph N. Gleason made certain adjustments of the gross agricultural production to obtain the supply of various products available for human consumption. For seeds, his coefficients of estimation for individual products were as follows: seeds required for rice, wheat, Indian corn, millet, barn-yarn millet, soybeans, and peanuts are estimated as 50 kg. per hectare; sorghum 30 kg. per hectare; other beans 75 kg. per hectare; and sweet potatoes 480 kg. per hectare. The portion of individual crops used for feed was estimated at 3 percent of the total rice production before 1935 and 4 percent after 1954. For Indian corn, 37 percent of the total production was used for feed and 30 percent for millet. He estimated that 35 percent of the total sweet potatoes production was used for feed each year before 1947 and 45 percent after 1947. His coefficients of estimation are adopted here and extend for the whole period to derive the seed and feed series. It is then a simple matter to obtain gross output series.

Estimates of gross output for individual products

1. *Food crops*

   Indian corn. Production data for 1901 through 1927 are lacking. Estimates are made as follows: 1901–1903, 4.32 percent of food production valued at 1952–1956 prices; 4.78 percent for 1904–1909; 5.24 percent for 1910–1914; 5.70 percent for 1915–1920; and 6.16 percent for 1921–1927.[1]

   Arrow root. The 1919–1928 average production is used for years before 1919.

---

1. The method of estimation used here is cruel; however, the effect on the total output is negligible since the production of Indian corn was a small fraction of the total, less than 0.1 percent in value terms.

2. *Special crops*

   Sugar cane. Sugar cane production of 1901 is estimated from sugar exports of 1901 with the assumption that the proportion of sugar produced and exported in 1901 is the same as in 1902.

3. *Fruits*

   Betel nut. 1921–1930 average is used as annual production estimates for 1909–1920.

   Guava. 1928–1932 average is used for years from 1909–1927.

   Mango. 1916–1920 average is used for 1909 through 1915.

   Papaya. 1921–1925 average used for 1909 through 1920.

   Wax-apple. 1928–1932 average taken for 1909–1927.

   Loquat and grape. Same as wax-apple.

   Total fruit production for 1901–1908 is estimated to be 2.7 percent of the gross value of agricultural production in each corresponding year valued at 1952–1956 average prices, exclusive of vegetables.

4. *Vegetables*

   Other root vegetables, other fruit vegetables, other stem vegetables and Chinese cabbage. The 1922–1925 average is used for 1918 through 1927.

   Potatoes. The 1928–1932 average is taken as the estimate for 1918–1927.

   Scallion, kidney beans, oriental pickling melons, celery, and wax-gourd. The 1919–1920 average is used for 1918.

   Water convolvulus. The 1921–1923 average is used for 1918 through 1920.

   Other leaf vegetables and other flower vegetables. The 1923 average is taken as the estimate for 1918 through 1921.

   For vegetables as a group, the gross value of production for 1901–1917 is estimated to be 2.5 percent of the gross value of agricultural production valued at 1952–1956 prices.

5. *Livestock and poultry products*

   Data on number of cattle, swine, and goats slaughtered are available for 1901–1910, but no data is available on the total weights. Average weight is estimated to be 136 kg. per head, which is the 1911–1920 average; swine is estimated to be 59 kg. per head; goats 15 kg. per head. The 1901–1910 average number of chickens is used as the estimate for 1904–1905.

TABLE A-1

Agricultural Products Used as Seeds and Feeds, 1901–1960

Unit: Metric Ton

Year	Rice	Wheat	Corn	Millet	Barn-Yarn Millet	Sorghum	Soybean
1901	30,800	100	33	2,600	200	—	—
1902	29,300	200	33	2,600	200	—	—
1903	35,500	200	33	2,700	200	—	—
1904	39,600	300	33	4,100	200	—	—
1905	41,000	300	226	400	300	—	—
1906	39,900	300	226	4,900	300	—	—
1907	42,900	300	226	900	300	—	—
1908	43,900	300	226	1,800	200	—	—
1909	43,700	300	226	600	300	—	—
1910	40,700	300	228	2,300	300	—	—
1911	43,100	300	228	2,000	300	—	—
1912	41,400	300	228	1,600	300	—	—
1913	46,700	300	228	2,000	300	—	900
1914	44,700	300	228	1,800	300	—	900
1915	45,100	300	333	1,600	300	—	900
1916	43,500	300	333	1,300	300	—	900
1917	44,000	300	333	1,400	300	—	800
1918	44,000	300	333	1,100	300	—	900
1919	46,000	300	333	900	300	—	900
1920	45,800	300	338	1,000	300	—	700
1921	46,100	300	338	700	300	—	600
1922	48,900	200	338	900	300	—	700
1923	46,200	200	338	900	300	—	600
1924	52,600	100	338	900	300	—	600
1925	55,100	100	447	700	300	—	500
1926	55,000	—	447	600	300	—	500
1927	58,800	—	447	500	300	—	500
1928	58,300	—	447	600	300	—	500
1929	56,200	—	447	400	300	—	500
1930	62,300	—	700	400	300	—	400
1931	63,700	—	700	400	300	—	400
1932	71,600	—	700	500	300	—	400
1933	69,600	—	700	500	300	—	400
1934	72,300	—	700	500	300	—	400
1935	73,000	100	800	500	300	—	400

TABLE A-1 (Continued)

Year	Rice	Wheat	Corn	Millet	Barn-Yarn Millet	Sorghum	Soybean
1936	75,100	—	800	500	300	—	400
1937	72,500	—	800	400	—	700	400
1938	73,400	100	800	400	—	700	300
1939	70,500	200	800	400	—	700	200
1940	65,800	300	900	400	—	800	200
1941	68,300	500	900	400	—	900	200
1942	65,900	500	900	400	—	900	300
1943	64,300	300	900	400	—	600	200
1944	62,300	300	900	300	—	400	400
1945	37,500	100	700	100	—	500	400
1946	46,100	100	3,100	2,500	—	300	400
1947	63,900	300	3,300	1,400	200	600	400
1948	67,900	400	3,000	1,700	—	100	1,000
1949	73,800	700	2,200	1,900	300	200	1,000
1950	95,400	900	2,700	1,600	100	300	1,000
1951	113,700	700	2,700	1,800	300	300	1,200
1952	102,100	700	2,900	2,100	200	400	1,200
1953	104,600	700	3,300	1,700	200	500	1,400
1954	106,600	600	4,500	1,700	100	500	1,500
1955	102,100	600	3,900	1,900	—	400	1,700
1956	110,800	800	4,300	2,000	—	600	1,900
1957	112,800	1,000	3,800	2,000	—	1,000	2,000
1958	114,700	1,100	5,100	1,800	—	1,000	2,400
1959	113,000	1,100	6,900	2,000	—	1,100	2,700
1960	114,800	1,300	8,400	2,000	—	1,000	3,000

Year	Sweet Potatoes	Cassava	Peanuts	Other Beans	Barley
1901	109,100	—	600	800	—
1902	134,600	—	600	800	—
1903	222,800	—	800	1,000	—
1904	281,800	—	900	1,600	100
1905	286,800	—	1,000	1,500	100
1906	284,100	—	900	1,500	100
1907	304,400	—	1,000	1,800	100
1908	365,100	—	1,000	2,100	100
1909	326,200	—	1,100	1,900	100
1910	273,800	—	1,000	2,000	100

TABLE A-1 (Continued)

Year	Sweet Potatoes	Cassava	Peanuts	Other Beans	Barley
1911	287,400	—	900	2,500	100
1912	288,500	—	900	2,500	100
1913	344,000	—	900	1,200	100
1914	342,100	—	1,000	1,400	100
1915	342,100	—	1,000	1,400	100
1916	302,800	—	1,000	1,300	100
1917	308,500	—	1,100	1,300	100
1918	341,000	—	1,200	1,300	100
1918	407,000	—	1,200	1,200	100
1920	347,100	—	1,100	1,000	100
1921	370,300	—	1,200	1,100	100
1922	390,100	—	1,200	1,000	100
1923	403,600	—	1,200	1,000	100
1924	450,200	—	1,300	900	—
1925	459,900	—	1,300	900	—
1926	465,500	—	1,300	1,000	—
1927	506,200	—	1,300	900	—
1928	511,500	—	1,300	900	—
1929	472,600	—	1,300	600	—
1930	525,600	—	1,300	700	—
1931	567,000	—	1,400	800	—
1932	564,300	—	1,400	800	—
1933	559,000	—	1,500	800	—
1934	614,300	—	1,500	800	—
1935	634,700	18,300	1,500	800	—
1936	669,700	18,300	1,500	800	—
1937	686,200	19,600	1,600	500	—
1938	668,800	17,700	1,600	800	—
1939	508,300	17,700	1,500	700	100
1940	592,900	24,900	1,500	800	100
1941	661,000	17,200	1,200	1,000	100
1942	617,500	10,400	900	800	100
1943	569,500	7,800	800	600	100
1944	614,300	6,700	1,000	700	100
1945	466,200	7,100	1,200	600	200
1946	532,200	18,500	2,600	700	100
1947	891,400	44,400	3,200	1,100	200
1948	1,083,000	50,000	3,900	900	100
1949	1,083,000	50,000	3,900	900	100
1950	1,100,400	44,900	4,100	1,300	100

TABLE A-1 (Continued)

Year	Sweet Potatoes	Cassava	Peanuts	Other Beans	Barley
1951	1,010,900	44,400	4,200	1,400	100
1952	1,045,300	43,700	4,000	1,600	—
1953	1,138,400	51,400	4,100	1,600	—
1954	1,278,400	46,900	4,700	2,000	—
1955	1,214,600	45,500	4,800	2,600	—
1956	1,266,100	42,200	4,900	2,400	—
1957	1,321,800	46,600	5,200	2,400	—
1958	1,440,800	54,400	5,200	2,500	—
1959	1,411,100	51,500	5,000	2,500	—
1960	1,453,400	55,600	5,000	1,900	—

Source: See the text of this Appendix.

ADJUSTED AGRICULTURAL POPULATION

TABLE B-1

Agricultural Population, 1901–1960

Year	Agricultural Population		Agricultural Population by Sex[b]		Agricultural Population of Working Age[c]	
	Unadjusted	Adjusted[a]	Male	Female	Male	Female
1901	1,786,744	1,988,566	1,052,349	936,217	767,583	684,843
1902	1,896,931	2,015,286	1,066,489	948,797	775,444	691,198
1903	2,105,962	2,032,272	1,075,478	956,794	779,506	694,154
1904	2,059,795	2,059,795	1,090,044	969,751	787,557	700,645
1905	1,961,556	2,094,921	1,108,932	986,289	798,653	709,635
1906	1,978,902	2,110,537	1,118,374	992,163	802,881	710,885
1907	2,030,227	2,159,912	1,143,673	1,016,239	818,412	725,086
1908	2,044,497	2,172,093	1,148,386	1,023,707	819,144	727,344
1909	1,973,705	2,099,472	1,108,521	990,951	788,158	701,098
1910	2,086,955	2,208,046	1,163,861	1,044,185	824,828	735,628
1911	2,124,459	2,244,742	1,181,408	1,063,334	828,758	745,929
1912	2,161,963	2,281,163	1,198,523	1,082,640	843,880	756,224
1913	2,199,468	2,317,491	1,215,756	1,101,752	853,218	766,257
1914	2,226,159	2,344,874	1,227,776	1,117,098	858,829	773,590
1915	2,252,850	2,372,083	1,234,906	1,137,177	860,729	783,970
1916	2,279,541	2,409,361	1,250,940	1,158,421	872,906	799,890
1917	2,285,372	2,426,857	1,257,597	1,169,260	878,557	808,660
1918	2,291,203	2,443,495	1,264,753	1,178,742	884,568	816,514
1919	2,297,035	2,461,433	1,272,950	1,188,283	891,319	824,430
1920	2,261,856	2,437,347	1,261,571	1,175,776	884,866	817,399
1921	2,226,677	2,403,891	1,243,292	1,160,599	872,791	807,777
1922	2,220,302	2,398,746	1,238,712	1,160,034	870,319	808,312
1923	2,262,891	2,442,611	1,259,410	1,183,201	885,617	825,401

TABLE B-1 (Continued)

Year	Agricultural Population Unadjusted	Agricultural Population Adjusted[a]	Agricultural[b] Population by Sex Male	Agricultural[b] Population by Sex Female	Agricultural Population of Working Age[c] Male	Agricultural Population of Working Age[c] Female
1924	2,305,323	2,485,987	1,279,786	1,206,201	900,713	842,411
1925	2,339,647	2,522,965	1,296,299	1,226,666	913,632	857,808
1926	2,377,047	2,565,412	1,314,774	1,247,638	914,819	861,369
1927	2,401,816	2,589,174	1,327,470	1,261,704	911,706	858,851
1928	2,458,259	2,647,765	1,356,980	1,290,785	919,761	868,182
1929	2,489,247	2,681,204	1,373,581	1,307,623	906,288	867,869
1930	2,534,404	2,729,521	1,398,061	1,331,460	922,440	871,574
1931	2,583,359	2,781,283	1,423,182	1,358,101	934,604	885,482
1932	2,576,003	2,776,652	1,419,980	1,356,672	928,100	881,023
1933	2,638,142	2,841,574	1,452,613	1,388,961	944,925	898,380
1934	2,700,990	2,907,230	1,486,467	1,420,763	962,339	915,255
1935	2,790,331	2,998,704	1,531,438	1,467,266	986,858	941,398
1936	2,854,733	3,065,720	1,565,663	1,500,057	1,004,372	960,336
1937	2,880,410	3,094,675	1,578,903	1,515,772	1,008,287	968,275
1938	2,896,397	3,113,057	1,586,103	1,526,954	1,008,286	973,280
1939	2,924,781	3,114,107	1,600,979	1,543,128	1,013,099	981,429
1940	2,984,258	3,207,301	1,630,592	1,576,709	1,022,122	1,000,579
1941	3,069,989	3,296,220	1,676,787	1,619,433	1,054,699	1,026,720
1942	3,186,870	3,416,347	1,736,871	1,679,476	1,031,276	1,063,612
1943	3,271,131	3,502,953	1,781,252	1,721,701	1,117,914	1,089,320
1944	3,318,235	3,538,235	1,792,116	1,746,119	1,123,478	1,103,547
1945	3,365,688	3,585,688	1,808,980	1,776,708	1,132,783	1,121,813
1946	3,522,880	3,792,969	1,874,309	1,855,660	1,172,380	1,170,365
1947	3,578,175	3,797,451	1,912,776	1,884,675	1,195,102	1,187,534
1948	3,779,652	4,012,109	2,026,516	1,985,593	1,264,749	1,249,931

TABLE B-1 (Continued)

Year	Agricultural Population		Agricultural[b] Population by Sex		Agricultural Population of Working Age[c]	
	Unadjusted	Adjusted[a]	Male	Female	Male	Female
1949	3,879,581	4,115,610	2,095,257	2,020,353	1,306,183	1,270,600
1950	3,998,470	4,231,556	2,158,940	2,072,616	1,344,372	1,302,017
1951	4,160,610	4,399,642	2,246,017	2,153,625	1,397,022	1,351,615
1952	4,257,136	4,498,350	2,300,006	2,198,344	1,428,994	1,378,362
1953	4,381,816	4,605,404	2,361,651	2,243,753	1,465,641	1,405,262
1954	4,488,763	4,704,990	2,412,719	2,292,271	1,495,644	1,434,274
1955	4,603,138	4,820,650	2,468,173	2,352,477	1,528,293	1,470,298
1956	4,698,532	4,920,970	2,513,635	2,407,339	1,553,675	1,503,142
1957	4,790,084	5,006,080	2,553,102	2,452,980	1,576,285	1,530,169
1958	4,880,901	5,101,653	2,602,353	2,499,300	1,604,871	1,557,564
1959	4,975,233	5,196,473	2,658,516	2,537,957	1,637,646	1,580,132
1960	5,373,375	5,593,375	2,863,248	2,730,127	1,761,756	1,698,138

a. The adjusted agricultural population is obtained by adding farm-hired laborers and their families to the unadjusted agricultural population series as recorded in the household registration records. The ratio of farm-hired labor population to total population is computed for 1905, 1915, 1920, and 1947. These ratios are 4.27 percent, 3.34 percent, 4.67 percent, and 3.40 percent, respectively. Assuming that the rate of change in the farm-hired population is constant, the ratio of farm-hired labor population to the total population can be established by interpolation and extrapolation for other years. Multiplying the total population each year by this ratio, one obtains farm-hired labor population for each year. Official data on farm-hired labor population for 1947–1960 are used.

b. Sex ratio in agriculture is assumed to be the same as the sex ratio for the total population.

c. Population of working age in agriculture is obtained by multiplying the agricultural population by the ratio of population with age above 12 to the total population. The ratio is estimated from Table 15 by assuming that the rate of change in age distribution between any pair of years is constant.

Source: Data on the unadjusted agricultural population of the period 1901–1944 are taken from *Statistical Summary*, Table 194; for 1946–1956 from *Agricultural Statistics, 1901–1955*, p. 7; 1957–1960 from *Agricultural Yearbook*, 1962 edition, p. 25. Data on farm-hired labor are drawn from *Statistical Abstract*, No. 15.

[*Appendix C*]

PRODUCTION OF MAJOR FARM PRODUCTS, 1901–1960

TABLE C-1

Rice Production

Year	Total, metric tons	Value, current prices	Value, 1952–1956 prices	Product Retained on Farms, [a] 1952–1956 prices	Gross Output, [b] 1952–1956 prices
			millions of Taiwan dollars		
1901	437,977	17.4	1,060.9	74.6	986.3
1902	403,061	20.2	976.3	71.0	905.3
1903	525,316	30.4	1,272.4	86.0	1,186.4
1904	594,266	23.9	1,439.4	95.9	1,343.5
1905	621,978	28.9	1,506.6	99.3	1,407.3
1906	566,940	32.1	1,373.3	96.6	1,276.7
1907	644,592	49.5	1,561.4	103.9	1,457.5
1908	665,232	38.3	1,611.4	106.3	1,505.1
1909	661,421	34.2	1,602.1	105.8	1,496.3
1910	598,211	35.6	1,449.0	98.6	1,350.4
1911	641,516	50.8	1,553.9	104.4	1,449.5
1912	578,087	54.6	1,400.3	100.3	1,300.0
1913	732,331	65.3	1,773.9	113.1	1,660.8
1914	658,322	44.3	1,594.6	108.3	1,486.3
1915	683,511	37.2	1,655.6	109.2	1,546.4
1916	664,167	42.5	1,608.8	105.4	1,503.4
1917	690,545	64.7	1,672.7	106.6	1,566.1
1918	661,744	93.3	1,602.9	106.6	1,496.3
1919	703,320	132.2	1,703.6	111.4	1,592.2
1920	691,764	109.0	1,675.6	110.9	1,564.7
1921	710,899	88.1	1,722.0	111.7	1,610.3
1922	777,831	80.6	1,884.1	118.4	1,765.7
1923	695,155	85.7	1,683.8	111.9	1,571.9
1924	868,090	130.7	2,102.7	127.4	1,975.3
1925	920,452	162.4	2,229.6	133.5	2,096.1
1926	887,739	144.1	2,150.3	133.2	2,017.1
1927	985,524	130.8	2,387.2	142.4	2,244.8
1928	970,715	134.0	2,351.3	141.2	2,210.1
1929	925,824	127.9	2,242.6	136.1	2,106.5
1930	1,052,931	107.2	2,550.4	150.9	2,399.5
1931	1,068,549	85.2	2,588.3	154.3	2,434.0
1932	1,278,458	134.9	3,096.7	173.4	2,923.3
1933	1,194,549	124.9	2,893.5	168.6	2,724.9

TABLE C-1 (Continued)

Year	Total, metric tons	Value, current prices	Value, 1952–1956 prices	Product Retained on Farms, [a] 1952–1956 prices	Gross Output,[b] 1952–1956 prices
			millions of Taiwan dollars		
1934	1,298,412	165.2	3,145.1	175.1	2,970.0
1935	1,303,164	197.3	3,156.6	176.8	2,979.8
1936	1,365,484	213.9	3,302.7	181.9	3,120.8
1937	1,319,018	208.8	3,195.0	175.6	3,019.4
1938	1,402,414	237.9	3,397.0	177.8	3,219.2
1939	1,307,391	241.7	3,166.8	170.8	2,996.0
1940	1,128,784	213.4	2,734.2	159.4	2,574.8
1941	1,199,006	246.3	2,904.3	165.4	2,738.9
1942	1,171,182	248.1	2,836.9	159.6	2,677.3
1943	1,125,804	256.8	2,727.0	155.8	2,571.2
1944	1,068,121	319.3	2,587.2	150.9	2,436.3
1945	638,828	535.4	1,547.4	90.8	1,356.6
1946	894,021	28,040.3	2,165.5	111.7	2,053.8
1947	999,012	64,855.0	2,419.8	154.8	2,265.0
1948	1,068,421	551,126.5	2,588.0	164.5	2,423.5
1949	1,214,524	626.0	2,941.9	178.8	2,763.1
1950	1,421,486	1,255.1	3,443.2	231.1	3,212.1
1951	1,484,792	1,507.7	3,596.5	275.4	3,321.1
1952	1,570,115	2,932.9	3,803.2	247.3	3,555.9
1953	1,641,557	4,582.2	3,976.2	253.4	3,722.8
1954	1,695,107	3,531.4	4,106.0	258.2	3,847.8
1955	1,614,953	4,357.2	3,911.8	247.3	3,664.5
1956	1,789,829	4,786.0	4,335.4	268.4	4,067.0
1957	1,839,009	5,447.1	4,454.5	273.2	4,181.3
1958	1,894,127	5,679.8	4,588.0	277.8	4,310.2
1959	1,856,316	6,021.5	4,496.4	273.7	4,222.7
1960	1,912,018	9,394.1	4,631.4	278.1	4,353.3

a. See Appendix A for the estimates of retained products as seeds and feeds.

b. Gross output is total production net of retained product on farms.

Source: (1) Data of total (physical) production and value of total production in current prices are taken from *Food Statistics*, Tables 2–1 and 2–5. (2) Data of rice price for 1952 through 1956 are taken from *Agricultural Yearbook*.

TABLE C-2

Sweet Potato Production

Year	Total, metric tons	Value, current prices	Value, 1952–1956 prices	Product Retained on Farms,[a] 1952–1956 prices	Gross Out-Put,[b] 1952–1956 prices
			millions of Taiwan dollars		
1901	238,999	2.8	70.8	32.3	38.5
1902	300,696	1.8	89.1	39.9	49.2
1903	538,773	2.6	159.6	65.8	93.8
1904	681,096	3.0	210.7	83.5	118.2
1905	684,237	5.7	202.6	84.9	117.7
1906	682,463	4.3	202.1	84.1	118.0
1907	725,303	4.4	214.8	90.2	124.6
1908	880,687	8.4	260.8	108.1	152.7
1909	786,219	9.4	232.9	96.9	136.0
1910	642,332	8.9	190.2	81.1	109.1
1911	677,930	7.6	200.8	85.1	115.7
1912	673,060	7.8	199.3	85.4	113.9
1913	822,582	7.5	243.6	101.9	141.7
1914	821,162	5.8	243.2	101.3	141.9
1915	809,680	4.4	239.8	99.6	140.2
1916	717,849	4.8	212.6	89.7	122.9
1917	734,140	10.1	217.4	91.4	126.0
1918	815,456	18.9	241.5	101.0	140.5
1919	998,702	26.6	295.8	120.5	175.3
1920	836,852	18.2	247.8	102.8	145.0
1921	892,361	15.9	264.3	119.7	144.6
1922	949,795	14.3	281.3	115.5	165.8
1923	986,312	15.6	292.1	119.5	172.6
1924	1,120,301	18.5	331.8	133.3	198.5
1925	1.145,349	22.4	339.2	136.2	203.0
1926	1,159,109	21.7	343.3	137.9	205.4
1927	1,275,048	21.4	377.6	149.9	227.7
1928	1,292,882	23.0	382.9	151.5	231.4
1929	1,180,858	22.8	349.7	140.0	209.7
1930	1,329,902	17.8	393.9	155.7	238.2
1931	1,442,813	13.4	427.3	167.9	259.4
1932	1,433,312	19.4	424.5	167.1	257.4
1933	1,413,469	20.5	418.6	165.6	253.0
1934	1,565,597	21.9	464.7	181.9	282.8
1935	1,624,101	25.4	481.0	188.0	293.0
1936	1,721,379	28.3	509.8	198.4	311.4
1937	1,769,985	26.6	524.2	203.2	321.0

TABLE C-2 (Continued)

Year	Total, metric tons	Value, current prices	Value, 1952–1956 prices	Product Retained on Farms,[a] 1952–1956 prices	Gross Output,[b] 1952–1956 prices
			millions of Taiwan dollars		
1938	1,726,188	29.5	511.3	198.1	313.2
1939	1,278,967	33.3	378.8	150.5	228.3
1940	1,512,420	43.2	447.9	175.6	272.3
1941	1,693,374	36.8	501.5	195.8	305.7
1942	1,556,390	39.2	461.0	182.9	278.1
1943	1,406,378	41.2	416.5	168.7	247.8
1944	1,528,170	53.2	452.6	181.9	270.7
1945	1,165,263	71.1	345.1	138.1	207.0
1946	1,330,506	3,394.6	394.1	157.6	236.5
1947	1,782,798	19,141.2	528.0	264.0	264.0
1948	2,002,865	262,951.9	593.2	296.6	296.6
1949	2,166,048	149.9	641.5	320.8	320.7
1950	2,200,833	227.0	651.8	325.9	325.9
1951	2,021,719	317.8	598.8	299.4	299.4
1952	2,090,463	515.4	619.2	309.6	309.6
1953	2,276,942	624.0	674.4	337.2	337.2
1954	2,556,823	648.2	757.3	378.6	378.7
1955	2,437,443	811.8	721.9	359.7	362.2
1956	2,568,104	959.4	760.6	375.0	385.6
1957	2,693,417	1,041.3	877.7	391.5	486.2
1958	2,957,893	1,251.2	876.1	426.7	449.4
1959	2,894,146	1,303.5	857.2	417.9	439.3
1960	2,978,676	1,832.0	882.2	430.5	451.7

a. See Appendix A for estimates of retained products as seeds and feeds.
b. Gross output is total production net of retained products.
Source: See Table C-1.

TABLE C-3

Peanut Production

Year	Total, metric tons	Value, current prices	Value, 1952–1956 prices	Product Retained on Farms,[a] 1952–1956 prices	Gross Output,[b] 1952–1956 prices
			millions of Taiwan dollars		
1901	5,771	0.4	18.4	1.9	16.5
1902	5,501	0.4	17.5	1.9	15.6
1903	8,937	0.7	28.4	2.5	25.9
1904	12,067	1.0	38.4	2.7	35.7
1905	10,926	0.9	34.7	3.2	31.5
1906	9,485	0.8	30.2	2.9	27.3
1907	12,196	1.0	38.8	3.2	35.6
1908	13,007	1.0	41.4	3.2	38.2
1909	18,952	1.5	60.3	3.5	56.8
1910	9,645	0.8	30.7	3.2	27.5
1911	8,686	0.7	27.6	2.9	24.7
1912	8,272	0.8	26.3	2.9	23.4
1913	11,109	1.3	35.3	2.9	32.4
1914	9,936	1.0	31.6	3.2	28.4
1915	12,083	1.1	38.4	3.2	35.2
1916	11,659	1.1	37.1	3.2	33.9
1917	13,827	1.8	44.0	3.5	40.5
1918	16,488	2.4	52.4	3.8	48.6
1919	17,870	2.9	56.8	3.8	53.0
1920	14,793	1.9	47.0	3.5	43.5
1921	17,482	1.9	55.6	3.8	51.8
1922	18,520	1.9	58.9	3.8	55.1
1923	17,792	1.7	56.6	3.8	52.8
1924	20,866	2.4	66.4	4.1	62.3
1925	21,618	2.9	68.7	4.1	64.6
1926	22,957	2.7	73.0	4.1	68.9
1927	23,748	2.6	75.5	4.1	71.4
1928	23,768	2.8	75.6	4.1	71.5
1929	19,393	2.3	61.7	4.1	57.6
1930	23,497	2.0	74.7	4.1	70.6
1931	25,446	1.7	80.9	4.4	76.5
1932	26,326	2.5	83.7	4.4	79.3
1933	24,018	2.3	76.4	4.8	71.6
1934	28,598	2.8	90.9	4.8	86.1
1935	29,339	3.5	93.3	4.8	88.5
1936	30,113	3.9	95.8	4.8	91.0
1937	31,705	4.1	100.8	5.1	95.7

TABLE C-3 (Continued)

Year	Total, metric tons	Value, current prices	Value, 1952–1956 prices	Product Retained on Farms,[a] 1952–1956 prices	Gross Output,[b] 1952–1956 prices
		millions of Taiwan dollars			
1938	28,095	3.9	89.3	5.1	84.2
1939	27,637	7.1	87.9	4.8	83.1
1940	28,671	7.7	91.2	4.8	86.4
1941	22,247	5.7	70.7	3.8	66.9
1942	12,907	2.9	41.0	2.9	38.1
1943	9,884	2.4	31.4	2.5	28.9
1944	12,185	7.6	38.7	3.2	35.5
1945	11,565	7.4	36.8	3.8	33.0
1946	37,379	487.1	118.9	8.3	110.6
1947	46,571	5,994.8	148.1	10.2	137.9
1948	53,348	17,975.6	169.6	11.8	157.8
1949	53,284	34.2	169.4	12.4	157.0
1950	57,110	68.1	181.6	13.0	168.6
1951	61,158	98.4	194.5	13.4	181.1
1952	60,037	134.7	190.9	12.7	178.2
1953	60,104	154.3	191.1	13.0	178.1
1954	65,868	199.7	209.5	14.9	194.6
1955	66,572	254.3	211.7	15.3	196.4
1956	81,847	347.0	260.3	15.6	244.7
1957	93,714	425.0	298.0	16.5	281.5
1958	96,423	450.0	306.6	16.5	290.1
1959	97,042	500.1	308.6	15.9	292.7
1960	102,167	660.0	324.9	15.9	309.7

a. See Appendix A for the estimates of seeds and feeds retained.
b. Gross output is obtained by subtracting retained product from total production.
Source: See Table C-1.

TABLE C-4

Sugar Cane Production

Year	Total, metric tons	Value, current prices [a]	Value, 1952–1956 prices
		millions of Taiwan dollars	
1901	552,676	—	62.5
1902	760,215	—	85.9
1903	409,895	—	46.3
1904	644,985	3.0	72.9
1905	693,567	3.2	78.4
1906	1,014,124	4.5	114.6
1907	830,189	3.9	93.8
1908	851,317	3.9	96.2
1909	1,271,683	5.4	143.7
1910	2,160,898	9.1	244.2
1911	2,829,153	11.1	319.8
1912	1,895,416	38.8	214.2
1913	918,311	18.9	103.8
1914	1,585,570	7.9	179.2
1915	2,360,284	11.8	266.8
1916	3,441,131	17.5	388.9
1917	5,092,870	25.9	575.6
1918	4,090,521	22.6	462.3
1919	3,378,803	22.4	381.9
1920	2,629,504	26.3	297.2
1921	2,962,994	38.9	334.9
1922	4,051,703	35.4	457.9
1923	3,979,118	31.0	449.7
1924	4,676,213	37.6	528.5
1925	5,303,900	47.9	599.4
1926	5,166,068	52.0	583.9
1927	4,452,289	45.7	503.2
1928	5,804,956	57.7	656.1
1929	7,375,167	72.9	833.5
1930	6,971,015	67.0	787.9
1931	6,566,802	56.5	742.2
1932	8,049,285	65.6	909.7
1933	5,286,720	29.0	597.5
1934	5,330,281	30.3	602.4
1935	8,086,356	55.2	913.9
1936	7,914,234	54.4	894.5
1937	8,563,125	64.3	967.8
1938	9,060,660	78.2	1,024.0
1939	12,835,395	117.7	1,450.6
1940	9,977,080	95.9	1,127.6

TABLE C-4 (Continued)

Year	Total, metric tons	Value, current prices [a]	Value, 1952–1956 prices
		millions of Taiwan dollars	
1941	8,392,385	84.3	948.5
1942	10,249,650	123.4	1,158.4
1943	10,092,283	111.3	1,140.6
1944	8,467,834	126.2	957.0
1945	4,159,279	65.0	470.1
1946	1,006,526	112.4	113.8
1947	796,012	7,960.1	90.0
1948	3,113,062	89,501.4	351.8
1949	6,193,818	275.1	700.0
1950	5,860,958	319.6	662.4
1951	3,584,997	422.7	405.2
1952	4,800,883	487.8	542.6
1953	8,394,348	1,134.4	948.7
1954	6,310,090	513.7	713.2
1955	6,088,871	703.6	688.2
1956	6,343,248	833.5	716.9
1957	7,083,395	1,024.1	800.6
1958	7,521,985	1,083.1	850.1
1959	8,093,447	1,373.3	914.7
1960	6,736,236	1,135.1	761.3

a. Data from 1901 through 1903 are not available.

Source: (1) Data of total production and the value of total production in current prices for years between 1901 and 1944 are taken from *Statistical Summary*, pp. 546–577; for 1945 through 1950 from *Agricultural Yearbook*, 1952 edition, p. 73; for 1951 through 1960 from *Agricultural Yearbook*, 1961 edition. (2) Sugar cane prices for 1952 through 1956 are taken from *Agricultural Yearbook*, 1961 edition.

TABLE C-5

Tea Production

Year	Total, metric tons	Value, current prices [a]	Value, 1952–1956 prices
		millions of Taiwan dollars	
1901	6,228	—	71.3
1902	7,659	—	87.7
1903	8,422	—	96.4
1904	6,637	—	76.0
1905	13,339	—	152.7
1906	12,717	1.7	145.6
1907	13,056	2.1	149.5
1908	13,035	1.9	149.2
1909	14,219	2.2	162.8
1910	13,766	3.8	157.6
1911	14,780	4.8	169.2
1912	13,427	4.7	153.7
1913	13,510	4.5	154.7
1914	13,634	4.4	156.1
1915	15,259	5.3	174.7
1916	15,102	5.2	172.9
1917	17,165	5.5	196.5
1918	17,131	6.9	196.1
1919	15,936	6.6	182.5
1920	9,040	3.2	103.5
1921	10,583	4.0	121.2
1922	11,216	5.4	128.4
1923	12,759	6.3	146.1
1924	12,376	6.5	141.7
1925	12,057	7.2	138.0
1926	11,937	7.5	136.7
1927	11,590	6.5	132.7
1928	11,006	6.3	126.0
1929	11,004	6.0	126.0
1930	10,444	3.8	119.6
1931	9,622	3.2	110.2
1932	8,823	2.6	101.0
1933	9,327	3.9	106.8
1934	11,035	7.5	126.3
1935	10,682	6.4	122.3
1936	10,849	7.4	124.2
1937	12,932	10.3	159.5
1938	13,102	9.2	150.0
1939	14,030	15.3	160.0
1940	11,685	16.9	133.8

TABLE C-5 (Continued)

Tea Production

Year	Total, metric tons	Value, current prices [a]	Value, 1952–1956 prices
		millions of Taiwan dollars	
1941	11,501	17.3	131.7
1942	11,586	17.4	132.6
1943	7,920	11.5	90.7
1944	4,283	7.6	49.0
1945	1,430	2.9	16.4
1946	2,919	135.9	33.4
1947	7,446	1,931.0	85.2
1948	8,452	10,877.7	96.8
1949	10,184	22.8	116.6
1950	9,645	36.6	110.4
1951	10,502	60.4	120.2
1952	11,582	106.4	132.6
1953	11,903	126.2	136.3
1954	13,006	177.4	148.9
1955	14,680	217.0	168.1
1956	13,420	121.3	153.6
1957	15,002	190.1	171.8
1958	15,764	206.0	180.5
1959	16,507	224.0	189.0
1960	17,365	248.1	198.8

a. Data for 1901 through 1905 are not available.
Source: See Table C-4.

TABLE C-6

Swine Slaughtered

Year	Total, metric tons	Value, current prices	Value, 1952–1956 prices
		millions of Taiwan dollars	
1901	18,959	4.7	171.9
1902	23,748	5.0	215.3
1903	29,745	5.9	269.7
1904	31,010	6.3	281.2
1905	32,900	6.9	298.3
1906	32,978	7.3	299.0
1907	33,297	7.5	301.9
1908	35,943	7.9	325.9
1909	37,622	9.0	341.1
1910	39,860	9.0	361.4
1911	35,362	9.8	320.6
1912	37,407	11.0	339.2
1913	39,388	12.1	357.1
1914	39,721	11.7	360.2
1915	42,256	11.8	383.1
1916	46,676	11.9	423.2
1917	47,367	14.5	429.5
1918	45,771	20.6	415.0
1919	49,684	27.7	450.5
1920	48,639	30.6	441.0
1921	50,353	24.2	456.6
1922	52,336	22.6	474.5
1923	54,464	22.7	493.8
1924	57,802	24.2	524.1
1925	60,611	29.8	549.6
1926	62,267	29.4	564.6
1927	67,894	29.9	615.6
1928	73,460	31.5	666.1
1929	71,172	30.9	645.3
1930	70,465	28.7	638.9
1931	78,637	21.6	713.0
1932	79,165	22.3	717.8
1933	74,416	24.1	674.7
1934	82,304	26.8	746.3
1935	89,652	31.0	812.9
1936	93,243	35.1	845.4
1937	95,934	37.3	869.8
1938	96,589	40.2	875.8
1939	88,544	54.1	802.8
1940	71,048	60.0	644.2

TABLE C-6 (Continued)

Swine Slaughtered

Year	Total, metric tons	Value, current prices	Value, 1952–1956 prices
		millions of Taiwan dollars	
1941	60,616	56.1	549.6
1942	55,251	64.8	501.0
1943	70,802	59.7	642.0
1944	28,580	36.0	259.0
1945	21,502	74.5	195.0
1946	18,198	1,637.8	165.0
1947	22,698	5,880.0	205.8
1948	38,626	52,398.7	350.2
1949	37,698	121.3	341.8
1950	60,891	299.5	552.1
1951	82,881	527.1	751.5
1952	93,966	673.1	852.0
1953	126,417	984.0	1,146.2
1954	130,612	1,092.6	1,184.3
1955	136,815	1,486.1	1,240.5
1956	146,916	1,640.0	1,332.1
1957	169,933	2,058.2	1,540.8
1958	193,911	2,284.6	1,758.2
1959	184,737	2,956.7	1,675.0
1960	175,100	3,550.4	1,587.7

Source: See Appendix A and Table C-4.

TABLE C-7

Cattle Slaughtered

Year	Total, metric tons	Value, current prices	Value, 1952–1956 prices
		millions of Taiwan dollars	
1901	1,551	0.3	12.7
1902	1,499	0.2	21.3
1903	1,926	0.4	15.8
1904	1,450	0.2	11.9
1905	1,443	0.3	11.8
1906	1,437	0.2	11.8
1907	1,892	0.3	15.5
1908	1,937	0.3	15.9
1909	2,243	0.3	18.4
1910	3,063	0.4	25.2
1911	4,267	0.6	35.0
1912	5,868	0.8	48.2
1913	5,187	0.7	42.6
1914	4,147	0.6	34.1
1915	3,917	0.5	32.2
1916	5,055	0.7	41.5
1917	4,059	0.7	33.3
1918	3,098	0.8	25.4
1919	2,259	0.8	18.6
1920	2,785	1.0	27.9
1921	3,711	1.0	30.5
1922	4,419	1.0	36.3
1923	4,325	1.0	35.5
1924	3,783	0.9	31.1
1925	3,194	0.9	26.2
1926	2,361	0.7	19.4
1927	2,417	0.7	19.8
1928	2,700	0.8	22.2
1929	2,859	0.8	23.5
1930	2,070	0.6	17.0
1931	2,408	0.6	19.8
1932	3,071	0.5	23.2
1933	2,470	0.5	20.3
1934	3,926	0.7	32.2
1935	3,341	0.7	27.4
1936	2,942	0.6	24.2
1937	3,896	0.9	32.0
1938	7,366	2.0	60.5
1939	4,784	1.8	39.3
1940	5,908	2.1	43.5

TABLE C-7 (Continued)

Cattle Slaughtered

Year	Total, metric tons	Value, current prices	Value, 1952–1956 prices
		millions of Taiwan dollars	
1941	4,158	2.6	34.2
1942	5,969	4.9	49.0
1943	2,181	2.1	17.9
1944	3,639	7.1	29.9
1945	2,546	3.9	20.9
1946	2,195	108.2	18.0
1947	2,439	209.5	20.0
1948	2,708	3,427.8	22.2
1949	2,565	3.7	21.1
1950	3,274	7.3	26.9
1951	5,796	24.2	47.6
1952	2,971	16.7	24.4
1953	3,060	23.8	25.1
1954	2,634	20.6	21.6
1955	2,908	28.7	23.9
1956	2,897	28.8	23.8
1957	2,924	28.6	24.0
1958	2,745	38.4	22.6
1959	2,874	43.4	23.6
1960	3,252	62.6	26.7

Source: See Appendix A and Table C-4.

[Appendix D]

CROP AREA AND FIXED CAPITAL SERIES

TABLE D-1

Crop Area   Unit: Hectare

Year	Total	Rice	Sugar Cane	Sweet Potatoes	Peanuts	Tea	Other Crops
1901	505,518	353,360	13,039	53,094	12,267	25,309	48,449
1902	515,388	344,989	16,921	61,247	12,939	27,456	51,837
1903	587,187	394,868	10,686	71,178	15,717	33,753	61,532
1904	669,986	435,134	13,963	90,486	18,991	31,736	80,676
1905	685,987	447,432	16,188	98,472	19,199	32,007	72,689
1906	706,727	458,591	22,735	94,124	18,391	32,786	81,100
1907	729,231	471,647	19,646	105,490	21,028	32,296	79,124
1908	753,934	478,953	18,562	118,466	21,127	33,335	83,491
1909	744,814	478,955	25,241	106,310	21,427	32,632	80,249
1910	731,431	456,276	41,005	102,203	19,166	32,572	80,209
1911	782,213	478,780	58,248	104,942	18,149	32,379	89,715
1912	782,976	480,204	51,246	110,225	18,015	34,034	89,252
1913	803,385	494,313	44,445	116,808	18,831	35,833	93,156
1914	814,399	499,678	50,006	113,939	19,279	36,713	94,724
1915	812,266	491,089	57,503	110,105	20,447	37,604	95,518
1916	814,305	471,677	75,844	107,456	20,880	43,032	95,416
1917	820,931	466,184	84,994	107,525	21,593	45,151	95,484
1918	858,613	483,344	97,861	115,794	23,565	45,518	92,531
1919	861,878	497,211	77,862	119,885	24,714	46,406	95,800
1920	829,797	500,169	70,081	112,825	22,835	37,806	86,081
1921	840,973	495,426	77,525	120,740	23,647	38,087	85,549
1922	873,422	511,241	91,844	120,240	23,758	38,496	87,843
1923	868,075	507,829	75,412	121,786	24,253	44,833	93,962
1924	900,550	531,450	79,688	121,110	25,261	45,770	97,271
1925	925,009	550,835	84,304	122,895	25,296	46,241	95,438
1926	939,347	567,172	80,153	124,515	26,292	45,878	95,337
1927	939,648	585,011	64,464	124,838	26,334	45,064	93,937
1928	944,439	584,918	69,995	122,817	26,239	45,221	95,250
1929	933,081	567,952	77,627	123,526	25,676	46,030	92,270
1930	976,396	614,390	70,741	125,180	26,712	45,653	93,720
1931	996,365	633,726	64,078	129,233	27,243	44,567	97,518
1932	1,042,974	664,325	70,815	130,718	28,421	44,221	104,474
1933	1,046,595	675,476	54,531	133,907	29,800	43,936	108,945
1934	1,053,352	666,979	58,590	138,163	30,772	44,389	114,099
1935	1,090,174	678,629	78,650	138,255	30,520	44,720	119,230
1936	1,102,972	681,548	82,983	140,110	30,735	44,682	122,914
1937	1,083,047	657,685	80,543	138,997	31,465	44,502	129,855
1938	1,060,453	625,398	86,785	134,561	31,087	44,463	138,159

TABLE D-1 (Continued)   *Unit: Hectare*

Year	Total	Rice	Sugar Cane	Sweet Potatoes	Peanuts	Tea	Other Crops
1939	1,092,233	626,131	108,205	126,401	29,335	44,798	157,363
1940	1,117,371	638,622	112,706	132,472	30,617	45,640	157,314
1941	1,129,148	646,927	104,796	142,245	24,789	44,763	165,628
1942	1,096,614	616,529	104,296	151,650	18,659	42,837	162,643
1943	1,071,256	610,051	104,331	160,979	17,194	39,571	139,130
1944	1,058,743	600,688	99,637	165,570	20,568	35,133	137,147
1945	867,819	502,018	71,784	134,715	24,626	34,255	100,421
1946	968,136	564,016	24,137	176,029	50,797	35,473	117,684
1947	1,182,991	677,557	19,937	213,403	65,106	39,439	167,549
1948	1,316,877	717,744	56,771	224,247	73,387	40,231	204,506
1949	1,396,665	747,675	81,595	234,164	77,059	40,830	213,342
1950	1,441,956	770,262	81,293	233,057	83,387	42,026	231,931
1951	1,455,406	789,075	52,833	231,389	84,889	42,704	254,516
1952	1,471,729	785,729	65,314	233,502	80,975	44,120	262,089
1953	1,466,224	778,384	75,487	237,788	82,580	44,655	247,330
1954	1,485,142	776,660	63,786	247,551	94,025	46,186	256,934
1955	1,466,909	750,739	52,123	245,513	96,034	47,000	275,500
1956	1,502,132	783,629	60,604	230,236	98,258	47,638	281,767
1957	1,525,943	783,267	65,491	228,760	103,584	48,006	296,835
1958	1,551,810	778,189	67,639	228,699	103,983	48,258	325,042
1959	1,553,958	776,050	66,149	226,487	99,135	48,442	337,695
1960	1,557,227	766,409	63,698	235,387	100,497	48,432	342,804

Source: See Table 17.

TABLE D-2

Cattle and Horses on Farms

Year	Cattle (*Unit: 1,000*)	Horses (*Unit: Head*)
1901	235	32
1902	256	82
1903	286	37
1904	325	68
1905	342	123
1906	353	263
1907	374	184
1908	415	167
1909	460	153
1910	480	198
1911	478	183
1912	446	183
1913	419	179
1914	404	137
1915	399	139
1916	386	147
1917	377	142
1918	385	152
1919	404	137
1920	429	176
1921	422	226
1922	409	189
1923	391	196
1924	383	218
1925	379	227
1926	381	224
1927	386	216
1928	388	279
1929	390	305
1930	391	325
1931	383	301
1932	367	333
1933	386	347
1934	395	411
1935	390	533
1936	371	637
1937	358	700
1938	325	700
1939	325	700
1940	300	700
1941	309	700
1942	312	700

TABLE D-2 (Continued)

Year	Cattle (Unit: 1,000)	Horses (Unit: Head)
1943	325	700
1944	331	2,311
1945	291	1,128
1946	280	772
1947	298	570
1948	310	474
1949	357	457
1950	365	379
1951	375	353
1952	383	323
1953	390	327
1954	406	446
1955	412	390
1956	414	295
1957	414	289
1958	419	250
1959	420	215
1960	420	202

Source: See Table 19.

[*Appendix E*]

PRICE INDEX AND EXPENDITURES
TABLE E-1

Implicit Price Index of Farm Products,[a]
1901–1960

| Year | Total Production | | Derived Price Index of Farm Products |
| | current prices | 1952–1956 constant prices | |
	millions of Taiwan dollars		
1901	26.8	1,405.3	1.91
1902	29.1	1,386.4	2.10
1903	42.5	1,881.0	2.26
1904	40.3	2,192.0	1.84
1905	48.3	2,234.7	2.16
1906	53.4	2,307.0	2.31
1907	71.3	2,498.6	2.85
1908	63.9	2,638.4	2.42
1909	65.7	2,717.7	2.42
1910	72.6	2,636.3	2.75
1911	90.2	2,786.4	3.24
1912	123.2	2,520.3	4.89
1913	116.3	2,871.7	4.05
1914	80.8	2,753.5	2.93
1915	77.6	2,964.2	2.62
1916	90.4	3,096.7	2.92
1917	130.7	3,355.6	3.89
1918	178.3	3,236.5	5.51
1919	235.6	3,312.2	7.11
1920	208.2	3,072.1	6.78
1921	192.9	3,244.7	5.94
1922	179.0	3,630.1	4.93
1923	186.1	3,534.4	5.26
1924	245.4	4,136.0	5.93
1925	299.9	4,363.4	6.87
1926	283.7	4,288.7	6.62
1927	264.0	4,534.3	5.82
1928	285.3	4,723.1	6.04
1929	293.3	4,727.0	6.20
1930	252.3	5,073.3	4.97
1931	203.8	5,196.7	3.92
1932	272.3	5,927.4	4.59
1933	230.3	5,365.5	4.29
1934	284.4	5,840.7	4.87

TABLE E-1 (Continued)

| Year | Total Production | | Derived Price Index of Farm Products |
| | current prices | 1952–1956 constant prices | |
	millions of Taiwan dollars		
1935	351.6	6,254.6	5.62
1936	378.0	6,498.7	5.82
1937	390.4	6,557.4	5.95
1938	445.4	6,837.8	6.52
1939	530.1	6,832.1	7.76
1940	516.8	5,947.8	8.69
1941	536.0	5,893.6	9.09
1942	595.5	5,950.8	10.01
1943	569.5	5,690.2	10.01
1944	685.2	4,871.3	14.07
1945	707.3	2,952.2	23.96
1946	38,969.0	3,478.1	1,120.41
1947	138,539.0	4,290.5	3,228.97
1948	1,233,758.0	5,041.8	24,470.58
1949	1,531.0	5,836.9	26.23
1950	2,878.0	6,588.1	42.30
1951	3,812.0	6,806.5	56.00
1952	5,837.0	7,362.3	79.28
1953	8,686.0	8,239.3	105.35
1954	7,430.0	8,317.7	89.33
1955	9,493.0	8,266.5	114.84
1956	10,570.0	8,992.6	117.54
1957	12,388.0	9,739.4	127.19
1958	13,707.0	10,327.2	132.73
1959	15,609.0	10,258.8	152.15
1960	20,655.0	10,460.8	197.45

a. The index here is derived by the series of value of total production in constant 1952–1956 farm prices divided into the series of value of total production in current prices. However, the series of current prices does not cover all products that are included in the output index compiled in this study because data for many products are not available for early years of this period. The coverage of the series of value of production in 1952–1956 constant prices is therefore consistently made to match the coverage of the series in current prices.

Source: Production series in current prices is compiled based on the data drawn from *Statistical Summary*, Tables 203, 204, 205, 206, 207, and 208 and from *Food Statistics*, for the period from 1901 to 1944; data for 1945 through 1960 are taken from *Statistical Abstract*, No. 15 and *Agricultural Yearbook*, 1961 edition.

TABLE E-2

Investment Expenditures for Irrigation,
1901–1960

Year	Government	Private [a]	Total	Total (deflated) [b]
		thousands of Taiwan dollars		*millions of Taiwan dollars*
1901	6.4	—	6.4	0.3
1902	35.7	—	35.7	1.7
1903	54.7	—	54.7	2.4
1904	67.5	—	67.5	3.7
1905	14.4	—	14.4	0.7
1906	36.6	120.0	156.6	6.8
1907	236.4	15.0	251.4	8.8
1908	137.8	70.0	207.8	8.6
1909	1,323.9	35.9	1,359.8	56.2
1910	960.6	—	960.6	34.9
1911	780.8	—	780.8	24.1
1912	854.7	—	854.7	17.5
1913	968.6	—	968.6	23.9
1914	—	—	—	—
1915	—	123.0	123.0	4.7
1916	413.7	—	417.3	14.3
1917	760.8	67.2	828.0	21.3
1918	696.1	58.0	754.1	13.7
1919	849.9	467.5	1,317.4	18.5
1920	2,375.2	82.5	2,454.7	36.2
1921	3,242.1	616.4	3,858.5	65.0
1922	3,197.3	287.9	3,485.2	70.7
1923	3,028.4	10,056.0	13,084.4	248.8
1924	2,031.2	2,948.7	4,979.9	84.0
1925	2,496.7	3,921.4	6,409.1	93.2
1926	1,400.0	6,544.8	7,944.8	120.0
1927	3,000.0	5,452.9	8,452.9	145.2
1928	6,015.0	16,322.6	22,337.6	369.8
1929	2,545.0	7,312.9	9,857.9	159.0
1930	3,607.2	3,076.2	6,683.4	134.5
1931	663.8	3,861.4	4,525.2	115.4
1932	580.8	1,346.5	1,927.3	42.0
1933	630.2	1,451.0	2,081.2	48.5
1934	1,029.6	2,130.6	3,160.2	64.9
1935	977.4	2,779.8	3,757.2	66.8
1936	—	434.6	434.6	7.5
1937	—	347.8	347.8	5.8
1938	80.0	391.6	471.6	7.2
1939	25.0	2,499.2	2,524.2	32.5
1940	4,206.4	2,763.8	6,970.2	80.2

TABLE E-2 (Continued)

Year	Government	Private [a]	Total	Total (deflated) [b]
		thousands of Taiwan dollars		millions of Taiwan dollars
1941	7,434.3	2,492.4	9,926.7	109.2
1942	5,873.4	3,507.1	9,380.5	93.7
1943	5,728.6	2,973.1	8,701.8	86.9
1944	9,488.3	3,131.2	12,619.6	89.7
1945	6,694.9	2,939.0	9,633.9	40.2
1946	—	27,471.3	27,471.3	2.4
1947	—	234,698.9	234,698.9	7.3
1948	—	1,578,423.4	1,578,423.4	6.4
1949	—	4,870.0	4,870.0	18.6
1950	449.7	9,349.9	9,799.6	23.2
1951	14,929.0	11,117.9	26,046.9	46.5
1952	24,040.9	15,483.6	35,524.5	49.8
1953	26,355.9	15,030.0	41,385.9	39.3
1954	27,494.8	9,197.6	36,692.4	41.1
1955	37,838.8	15,067.3	52,906.1	46.1
1956	41,117.3	54,044.6	95,161.9	81.0
1957	20,734.4	36,159.8	56,894.2	44.7
1958	56,755.0	84,576.6	141,331.6	106.5
1959				
1960 [c]	26,001.9	90,771.5	116,773.4	59.1

a. Primarily by local irrigation associations.
b. The deflator used here is shown in Table E-1.
c. Figure includes expenditures incurred from July 1, 1959, to June 30, 1960.
Source: Data are taken from E. L. Rada and T. H. Lee, *Irrigation Investment in Taiwan*, Tables B-1 and B-2. Figures shown here are rounded.

TABLE E-3

Investment Expenditures on Transportation,
1901–1960

Year	Current Prices	Constant Prices [a] millions of Taiwan dollars
1901	1,814,525	95.0
1902	1,764,945	84.0
1903	1,884,256	83.4
1904	1,965,572	106.8
1905	2,344,816	108.6
1906	2,512,382	108.8
1907	2,636,778	92.5
1908	2,657,870	109.8
1909	2,887,161	119.3
1910	3,400,776	123.7
1911	4,029,867	124.4
1912	5,126,193	104.8
1913	4,545,303	112.2
1914	4,604,586	157.2
1915	5,035,780	192.2
1916	5,066,980	173.5
1917	5,627,946	144.7
1918	7,029,426	127.8
1919	8,432,048	118.6
1920	15,165,754	223.7
1921	14,688,536	247.3
1922	13,842,673	280.8
1923	13,327,015	253.4
1924	13,214,400	222.8
1925	13,165,284	191.6
1926	13,905,968	210.0
1927	15,705,648	269.8
1928	16,833,141	278.7
1929	18,171,112	293.1
1930	17,812,933	358.4
1931	17,308,427	441.5
1932	16,698,627	363.8
1933	19,238,643	448.4
1934	21,759,188	446.8
1935	23,386,405	416.8
1936	26,580,412	456.7
1937	30,584,683	514.0
1938	38,876,459	596.3
1939	44,757,906	576.8
1940	54,142,000	623.0

TABLE E-3 (Continued)

Year	Current Prices	Constant Prices [a] *millions of Taiwan dollars*
1941	49,515,480	544.7
1942	49,592,926	495.4
1943	52,813,833	527.6
1944	57,947,734	411.8
1945 [b]	—	—
1951	6,000,000	10.7
1952	99,000,000	124.9
1953	80,000,000	75.9
1954	49,000,000	54.8
1955	57,000,000	49.6
1956	128,000,000	108.9
1957	102,000,000	80.2
1958	144,000,000	108.5
1959	175,000,000	115.0
1960	239,000,000	121.0

a. It is recognized that a general price index is more appropriate here. Since such an index is not available, the deflator used here is the derived index for farm products.

b. Data for years from 1945 through 1950 are not available.

Source: For 1901 through 1944 data are taken from *Statistical Summary*, Table 336; for 1951–1960 from Directorate-General of Budgets, Accounts, and Statistics, *National Income of the Republic of China*, Table 11.

TABLE E-4

Public Health Expenditures, 1901–1960

Year	Provincial Government	Local Governments [a]	Total [b]	Total (deflated) [c] millions of Taiwan dollars
1901	275,292	—	275,292	14.4
1902	251,505	—	251,505	12.0
1903	254,070	—	254,070	11.2
1904	251,117	—	251,117	13.6
1905	256,129	—	256,129	11.8
1906	276,393	—	276,393	12.0
1907	297,371	—	297,371	10.4
1908	325,533	—	325,533	13.4
1909	367,247	—	367,247	15.2
1910	408,565	—	408,565	14.8
1911	442,259	—	442,259	13.6
1912	490,428	—	490,428	10.0
1913	500,497	—	500,497	12.4
1914	556,645	—	556,645	19.0
1915	569,232	—	569,232	21.7
1916	588,463	—	588,463	20.2
1917	620,314	—	620,314	15.9
1918	714,706	—	714,706	13.0
1919	785,093	—	785,093	11.0
1920	1,019,918	750,736	1,770,654	26.1
1921	1,112,278	2,446,189	3,558,467	59.9
1922	1,032,899	3,096,200	4,129,099	83.8
1923	1,064,698	2,871,514	3,936,212	74.8
1924	1,066,890	2,905,267	3,972,157	67.0
1925	1,041,340	3,574,774	4,616,114	67.2
1926	1,066,567	3,376,515	4,443,082	67.1
1927	1,074,551	3,708,477	4,783,028	82.2
1928	1,089,381	4,125,619	5,215,000	86.3
1929	1,217,401	4,104,894	5,322,295	85.8
1930	1,195,935	4,266,353	5,462,288	109.9
1931	1,152,341	3,847,081	4,999,422	127.5
1932	1,122,249	3,842,162	4,964,411	108.2
1933	1,120,924	3,603,978	4,724,902	110.1
1934	1,219,999	4,264,223	5,484,222	112.6
1935	1,233,057	4,499,220	5,732,277	102.0
1936	1,273,280	4,673,200	5,946,480	102.2
1937	1,323,150	5,734,895	7,058,045	118.6
1938	981,821	5,711,010	6,692,831	102.6

TABLE E-4 (Continued)

Year	Provincial Government	Local Governments [a]	Total [b]	Total (deflated) [c] millions of Taiwan dollars
1939	979,838	5,693,376	6,673,214	86.0
1940	1,132,987	6,759,570	7,892,557	90.8
1941	1,241,962	7,789,955	9,031,917	99.4
1942	1,393,908	8,598,977	9,992,885	99.8
1943	1,561,688	9,662,595	11,224,283	112.1
1944	1,518,281	12,198,740	13,717,021	97.5
1945	—	—	—	—
1946	84,421,887	20,593,314	105,015,201	9.4
1947	340,642,747	35,147,978	375,790,725	11.6
1948	3,064,666,902	—	3,064,666,902	12.5
1949	3,107,134	645,373	3,752,507	14.3
1950	11,254,192	5,782,290	17,036,482	40.3
1951			25,000,000	44.6
1952			32,000,000	40.4
1953			46,000,000	43.7
1954			64,000,000	71.6
1955			64,000,000	55.7
1956			132,000,000	112.3
1957			154,000,000	121.1
1958			171,000,000	128.8
1959			183,000,000	120.3
1960			248,000,000	125.6

a. Data on expenditures for public health by local governments are not available for 1901 through 1919.

b. Total for 1951–1960 is not separated between the provincial and local governments.

c. See Table E-3, footnote a.

Source: See Table E-3.

BIBLIOGRAPHY

Abramovitz, Moses. "Resource and Output Trends in the United States since 1870," *American Economic Review,* papers and proceedings, XLVI (May 1956), 5–23.

Agarwala, A. N., and S. P. Singh (eds.). *The Economics of Underdevelopment.* London: Oxford University Press, 1958.

Anderson, W. A. *Farmers' Association in Taiwan.* A report to the Joint Commission on Rural Reconstruction, and Economic Cooperation Administration Mission to China. Taipei, Taiwan: Joint Commission on Rural Reconstruction, 1950.

Banerji, Hrishikes. *Technical Progress and the Process of Economic Development.* The Hague: Foundation for International Cooperation, Netherland Universities, 1956.

Barclay, George W. *A Report on Taiwan's Population to the Joint Commission on Rural Reconstruction.* Princeton, New Jersey: Office of Population Research, Princeton University, 1954.

————. *Colonial Development and Population in Taiwan.* Princeton, New Jersey: Princeton University Press, 1954.

Barlowe, Raleigh. "Land Reform and Economic Development," *Journal of Farm Economics,* XXXV (May 1953), 173–187.

Barger, Harold, and Hans H. Landsberg. *American Agriculture: 1899–1939.* New York: National Bureau of Economic Research, Inc., 1942.

Barton, Glen T., and Martin R. Cooper. "Relation of Agricultural Production to Inputs," *Review of Economics and Statistics,* XXX (May 1948), 117–126.

Brown, Lester R. *An Economic Analysis of Far Eastern Agriculture.* Washington, D. C.: U. S. Department of Agriculture, Economic Research Service, Regional Analysis Division, 1961.

Buck, John L. *Some Basic Agricultural Problems of China.* New York: International Secretariat, Institute of Pacific Relations, 1947.

————. *Land Utilization in China.* Shanghai, China: The Commercial Press, Ltd., 1937.

————. *Chinese Farm Economy: A Study of 2,866 Farms in 17 Localities and 7 Provinces in China.* Chicago: University of Chicago Press, 1930.

Chen, Cheng. *Land Reform in Taiwan.* Taipei, Taiwan: China Publishing Company, 1961.

Clark, Colin. *The Conditions of Economic Progress.* (3rd ed.) London: Macmillan & Company, 1957.

Denison, Edward F. *The Sources of Economic Growth in the United States and the Alternative Before Us.* (Supplementary Paper No. 13 of the

Committee for Economic Development.) New York: Committee for Economic Development, 1962.

Directorate-General of Budgets, Accounts and Statistics, Executive Yuan. *National Income of the Republic of China.* Taiwan: Directorate-General of Budgets, Accounts, and Statistics, 1962.

————. *Taiwan Economic Indicators.* No. 5. Taiwan: Directorate-General of Budgets, Accounts and Statistics, Executive Yuan, 1956.

Domar, Evsey D. "On the Measurement of Technological Change," *The Economic Journal,* LXXI (December 1961), 707–729.

Dore, R. P. "Agricultural Improvement in Japan, 1870–1900," *Economic Development and Cultural Change,* IX, No. 1, Part II (October 1960), 69–91.

Dovring, F. "The Share of Agriculture in a Growing Population," *Food and Agricultural Organization Monthly Bulletin* (August–September 1959), pp. 1–11.

Economic Stabilization Board, Executive Yuan, China. *A Review of the Economic Situation of the Republic of China: July 1954–June 1955.* Taiwan: Economic Stabilization Board, 1955.

Formosa Education Association. *Modern Formosa, with Special Reference to Education.* Taiwan: Formosa Education Association, 1923.

Georgescu-Roegen, Nicholas. "Economic Theory and Agrarian Economics," *Oxford Economic Papers,* XII (February 1960), 1–41.

Ginsburg, Norton Sydney. *The Economic Resources and Development of Formosa.* New York: International Secretariat, Institute of Pacific Relations, 1953.

Glass, Sheppard. "Some Aspects of Formosa's Economic Growth," *The China Quarterly,* No. 15 (July–September 1963), 12–34.

Gleason, Ralph N. *Taiwan Food Balance: 1935–54.* (Joint Commission on Rural Reconstruction Publications: Food and Fertilizer series, No. 5.) Taiwan: Joint Commission on Rural Reconstruction, 1956.

Grajdanzev, Andrew Jonah. *Formosa Today: An Analysis of the Economic Development and Strategic Importance of Japan's Tropical Colony.* New York: International Secretariat, Institute of Pacific Relations, 1942.

Griliches, Zvi. "Specification Bias in Estimates of Production Functions," *Journal of Farm Economics,* XXXIX (February 1957), 8–20.

————. "Hybrid Corn and the Economics of Innovation," *Science,* No. 132 (July 1960), 275–280.

————. "Research Costs and Social Returns: Hybrid Corn and Related Innovation," *Journal of Political Economy,* LIVI (October 1958), 419–431

————. "Research Expenditures, Education, and the Aggregate Agricultural Production Function," *American Economic Review,* LIV (December 1964), 961–974.

Heady, Earl O., and John L. Dillion. *Agricultural Production Functions.* Iowa: Iowa State University Press, 1961.

Heady, Earl O., and R. Shaw. "Resource Returns and Productivity Coefficients," *Journal of Farm Economics,* XXXVI (May 1954), 234–258.

Higgins, Benjamin H. *Economic Development: Problems, Principles, and Policies.* New York: W. W. Norton & Company, Inc., 1959.

Hirschman, Albert O. *The Strategy of Economic Development.* New Haven: Yale University Press, 1958.

Hsieh, R. Z. *Taiwan Ten-Year.* Taipei, Taiwan: Shih-Sen Pao (New Life Daily), 1955.

Hsieh, S. C., and T. H. Lee. *An Analytical Review of Agricultural Development in Taiwan: An Input-Output and Productivity Approach.* (Joint Commission on Rural Reconstruction Publications: Economic Digest series, No. 12.) Taiwan: Joint Commission on Rural Reconstruction, 1958.

Hsing, Mo-Huan, *et al. Relationships Between Agricultural and Industrial Development in Taiwan During 1950–59.* Taiwan: National Taiwan University, 1960.

Hsu, S. C. "Report on Rural Health Program in Taiwan, Republic of China." Taiwan: Joint Commission on Rural Reconstruction, 1962. (Mimeographed.)

Hughes, R. B. "Marginal Returns on Agricultural Resources in Southern Mountain Valley," *Journal of Farm Economics,* XXXVI (May 1954), 334–339.

International Cooperation Administration Mission to China. *Taiwan Gross Capital Formation: 1953–56.* Taiwan: International Cooperation Administration Mission to China, 1957.

Johansen, Leif. "A Method for Separating the Effects of Capital Accumulation and Shifts in Production Function Upon Growth in Labor Productivity," *The Economic Journal,* LXXI (December 1961), 775–782.

Johnston, Bruce F. "Agricultural Development and Economic Transformation: Japan, Taiwan, and Denmark," a paper presented for the Conference on Relations between Agriculture and Economic Growth, November 1960. Stanford, California: Food Research Institute, Stanford University, 1960. (Mimeographed.)

————. "Agricultural Productivity and Economic Development in Japan," *Journal of Political Economy,* LIX (December 1951), 498–513.

Johnston, Bruce F., and J. W. Mellor. "The Role of Agriculture in Economic Development," *American Economic Review,* LI (September 1961), 566–593.

Joint Commission on Rural Reconstruction, and the Faculty of Economics of National Taiwan University. *A Study of the Effects of the Population Trend on Economic Development in Taiwan.* Taiwan: Joint Commission on Rural Reconstruction, 1961.

Joint Commission on Rural Reconstruction. *General Agricultural Statistics of Taiwan with a Summary of JCRR Project Status : 1952–1955.* Taiwan: Joint Commission on Rural Reconstruction, 1956.

————. *General Report No. 1.* Taiwan: Joint Commission on Rural Reconstruction, 1950.

————. *General Report No. 7.* Taiwan: Joint Commission on Rural Reconstruction, 1956.

————. *Taiwan Agricultural Statistics: 1901–1955.* (Joint Commission on

Rural Reconstruction Publications: Economic Digest Series, No. 8.) Taiwan: Joint Commission on Rural Reconstruction, 1956.

Jorgenson, Dale W. "The Development of a Dual Economy," *The Economic Journal,* LXXI (June 1961), 309–334.

Kaldor, Nicholas. *Essays on Economic Stability and Growth.* Glencoe, Illinois: The Free Press, 1960.

Kayo, N. (ed.). *Basic Agricultural Statistics of Japan.* Tokyo, Japan: Agricultural, Forestry, and Fisheries Productivity Conference, 1958.

Kendrick, John W. *Productivity Trends: Capital and Labor.* New York: National Bureau of Economic Research, Inc., 1956.

———. *Productivity Trends in the United States.* (National Bureau of Economic Research General Series No. 71.) Princeton, New Jersey: Princeton University Press, 1961.

Kirby, Stuart F. *Rural Progress in Taiwan.* Taiwan: Joint Commission on Rural Reconstruction, 1960.

Klein, L. R. "The Estimation of Distributed Lags," *Econometrica,* XXVI (October 1958), 553–565.

Koyck, L. M. *Distributed Lags and Investment Analysis.* Amsterdam: North-Holland Publishing Company, 1954.

Kuznets, Simon S. *Six Lectures on Economic Growth.* Glencoe, Illinois: The Free Press, 1959.

Kuznets, Simon S., Wilbert Moore, and Joseph J. Spengler. *Economic Growth: Brazil, India, Japan.* Durham, N. C.: Duke University Press, 1955.

Lewis, W. Arthur. *The Theory of Economic Growth.* Homewood, Illinois: Richard D. Irwin, Inc., 1955.

Lockwood, William W. *The Economic Development of Japan: Growth and Structural Change, 1868–1938.* Princeton, New Jersey: Princeton University Press, 1954.

Ma, F. C. *A Preliminary Study of Farm Implements Used in Taiwan Province.* Taiwan: Joint Commission on Rural Reconstruction, 1955.

Meier, Gerald M. *Leading Issues in Development Economics.* New York: Oxford University Press, 1964.

Mellor, John W., and Robert D. Stevens. "The Average and Marginal Products of Farm Labor in Underdeveloped Economies," *Journal of Farm Economics,* XXXVIII, No. 3 (August 1956), 780–791.

Mills, Frederick C. *Productivity and Economic Progress.* New York: National Bureau of Economic Research, 1952.

Nicholls, William H. "Investment in Agriculture in Underdeveloped Countries," *American Economic Review,* XLV (May 1955), 58–73.

———. "An 'Agricultural Surplus' as a Factor in Economic Development," *Journal of Political Economy,* LXXI, No. 1 (February 1963), 1–29.

———. "The Place of Agriculture in Economic Development," a paper presented at a Round Table on Economic Development with particular reference to East Asia (sponsored by the International Economic Association), held at Gamagori, Japan, during April 2–9, 1960. Nashville, Tennessee: Vanderbilt University, 1960. (Mimeographed.)

Nurkse, Ragnar. *Problems of Capital Formation in Underdeveloped Countries.* Oxford: Basil Blackwell & Mott, Ltd., 1953.

Nutter, Warren. "On Measuring Economic Growth," *Journal of Political Economy,* LXV (February 1957), 51–63.

Ohkawa, Kazushi, and Henry Rosovsky. "The Role of Agriculture in Modern Japanese Economic Development," *Economic Development and Cultural Change,* IX, No, 1, Part II (October 1960), 43–67.

Ohkawa, Kazushi, *et al. The Growth Rate of Japanese Economy Since 1878.* Tokyo, Japan: Kinokuniya Bookstore Company, Ltd., 1957.

Ojala, E. M. *Agriculture and Economic Progress.* London: Oxford University Press, 1952.

Okun, Bernard, and Richard W. Richardson (eds.). *Studies in Economic Development.* New York: Holt, Rinehart and Winston, 1961.

Organization for Economic Co-operation and Development. *Policy Conference on Economic Growth and Investment in Education.* Vol. III. Washington, D. C.: Organization for Economic Co-operation and Development, 1962.

Proceedings of Agricultural Economics Seminar. (Agricultural Economics Seminar held at the College of Agriculture, National Taiwan University, Taipei, Taiwan, September 1958.) Taiwan: National Taiwan University, 1959.

Rada, E. L., and T. H. Lee. *Irrigation Investment in Taiwan: An Economic Analysis of Feasibility, Priority and Repayability Criteria.* (Joint Commission on Rural Reconstruction Publications: Economic Digest Series, No. 15.) Taiwan: Joint Commission on Rural Reconstruction, 1963.

Ranis, Gustav, and J. C. H. Fei. "A Theory of Economic Development," *American Economic Review,* LI (September 1961), 553–565.

Ranis, Gustav. "Investment Criteria, Productivity and Economic Development: An Empirical Comment," *Journal of Political Economy,* LXXVI (May 1962), 298–302.

Raper, Arthur F. *Rural Taiwan: Problem and Promise.* Taiwan: Joint Commission on Rural Reconstruction, 1953.

Raper, Arthur F., *et al. Urban and Industrial Taiwan.* Taiwan: Good Earth Press, Ltd., 1954.

Research Institute, Bank of Taiwan. *Agricultural Economy of Taiwan.* Taiwan: Bank of Taiwan, 1962.

Riggs, Fred W. *Formosa Under Chinese Nationalist Rule.* New York: American Institute of Pacific Relations, Inc., 1952.

Rosenstein-Rodan, P. N. "Programming on Theory and in Italy Practice." Cambridge, Mass.: Center for International Studies, Massachusetts Institute of Technology, December 1955. (Mimeographed.)

———. "Problems of Industrialization of Eastern and South-Eastern Europe," *The Economic Journal,* LIII (June–September 1943), 202–211.

———. "Notes on the Theory of the 'Big-Push,' " Cambridge, Mass.: Center for International Studies, Massachusetts Institute of Technology, March 1957. (Mimeographed.)

Rosovsky, Henry. *Capital Formation in Japan: 1868–1940.* New York: The Free Press of Glencoe, 1961.

Rostow, Walter W. *The Stages of Economic Growth*. Cambridge, England: Cambridge University Press, 1960.

Ruttan, Vernon W. "The Contribution of Technological Progress to Farm Output: 1950–75," *Review of Economics and Statistics*, XXXVIII, No. 1 (1956), 61–69.

Schmookler, Jacob. "The Changing Efficiency of the American Economy, 1869–1938," *Review of Economics and Statistics*, XXXIV (August 1952), 214–231.

Schultz, Theodore W. "Capital Formation by Education," *Journal of Political Economy*, LXVIII (December 1960), 571–583.

———. "Investment in Human Capital," *American Economic Review*, LI (March 1961), 1–18.

———. *Transforming Traditional Agriculture*. New Haven: Yale University Press, 1964.

———. *The Economic Organization of Agriculture*. New York: McGraw-Hill, 1953.

———. "The Supply of Food in Relation to Economic Development," *Economic Development and Cultural Change*, I (December 1952), 244–249.

———. "United States Endeavors to Assist Low-Income Countries Improve Economic Capabilities of Their People," *Journal of Farm Economics*, Proceedings Issue, XLIII, No. 5 (December 1961), 1068–1077.

———. "Reflections on Agricultural Production, Output and Supply," *Journal of Farm Economics*, XXXVIII (August 1956), 748–762.

Shen, T. H. *Agricultural Planning and Production*. Taiwan: Economic Stabilization Board, Executive Yuan, 1958.

———. *Economic Significance of Agricultural Development in Taiwan*. Taiwan: Economic Stabilization Board, Executive Yuan, 1955.

Shishido, Toshio. "Japanese Agriculture: Productivity Trend and Development of Technique," *Journal of Farm Economics*, XLIII, No. 2 (May 1961), 285–295.

Solow, Robert M. "Technical Change and the Aggregate Production Function," *Review of Economics and Statistics*, XXXIX (August 1957), 312–320.

———. "Technical Progress, Capital Formation and Economic Growth," *American Economic Review*, LII (May 1962), 76–86.

———. "On A Family of Lag Distribution," *Econometrica*, XXVIII (April 1960), 393–406.

Stigler, George J. *Trends in Output and Employment*. New York: National Bureau of Economic Research, 1947.

Svennilson, Ingvar. "Education, Research and Other Unidentified Factors in Growth." A paper presented to the International Congress on Economic Development held at Vienna, Austria, August 30–September 6, 1962. London: International Economic Association, 1962. (Mimegraphed.)

Taiwan, Bureau of Accounting and Statistics, Provincial Government of Taiwan. *Taiwan Statistical Abstract*. No. 15. Taiwan: Bureau of Accounting and Statistics, Provincial Government of Taiwan, 1955.

Taiwan, Bureau of Accounting and Statistics, Provincial Government of Taiwan. *Results of the Seventh Population Census of Taiwan: 1940.* Taiwan: Bureau of Accounting and Statistics, Provincial Government of Taiwan, 1953.

Taiwan, Committee on the Promotion of Rotational Irrigation. *Rotational Irrigation.* Taiwan: Committee on the Promotion of Rotational Irrigation, 1958. (Pamphlet)

Taiwan, Committee of Sample Census of Agriculture. *A Report on the 1956 Sample Census of Agriculture.* Taiwan: Committee of Sample Census of Agriculture, 1959.

Taiwan, Department of Agriculture and Forestry. *Agriculture and Forestry Progress.* Taiwan: Department of Agriculture and Forestry, Taiwan Provincial Government, 1950.

———. *Taiwan Agricultural Yearbook.* (1960, 1961, and 1962 editions.) Taiwan: Department of Agriculture and Forestry, Provincial Government of Taiwan.

Taiwan, Department of Statistics. *Statistical Summary of Taiwan for the Past 51 Years.* Taiwan: Department of Statistics, 1946.

———. *Life Table of Taiwan: 1936–40.* Taiwan: Department of Statistics, 1947.

Taiwan, Economic Research Center. *Taiwan Statistical Data Book.* Taiwan: Economic Research Center, Council for U. S. Aid, Executive Yuan, 1962.

Taiwan Provincial Food Bureau. *Taiwan Food Statistics Book.* (1958, 1959, 1960, 1961, 1962, and 1963 editions.) Taiwan: Taiwan Provincial Food Bureau.

Takekoshi, Yosaburo. *Japanese Rule in Formosa.* Translated by George Braithwaite. London: Longmans, Green, and Co., 1907.

Tang, Anthony M. "Agriculture and Economic Development in Underdeveloped Countries with Particular Reference to Mainland China." Nashville, Tennessee: Department of Economics and Business Administration, Vanderbilt University, 1961. (Mimeographed research proposal.)

———. "Research and Education in Japanese Agricultural Development: 1880–1938," *Economic Studies Quarterly,* XIII (Part I: February 1963; Part II: May 1963), 27–41; 91–99.

———. *Economic Development in the Southern Piedmont: 1860–1950.* Chapel Hill, N. C.: University of North Carolina Press, 1958.

Tang, Hui-Sun. *Land Reform in Free China.* Taiwan: Joint Commission on Rural Reconstruction, 1957.

Tsui, Y. C. *A Summary Report on Farm Income of Taiwan in 1957 in Comparison with 1952.* Taiwan: Joint Commission on Rural Reconstruction, 1959.

Tsui, Y. C., and S. C. Hsieh. *Farm Income of Taiwan.* Taiwan: Joint Commission on Rural Reconstruction, 1954.

U. S. Office of Naval Operations. *Civil Affairs Handbook: Taiwan-Economic Supplement.* OPNAV 50 E-13. Washington, D. C., 1944.

Viner, Jacob. *International Trade and Economic Development.* Glencoe, Illinois: The Free Press, 1952.

Weisbrod, Burton A. "Education and the Investment in Human Capital," *Journal of Political Economy,* Supplement, LXX (October 1962), 106–123.

Yen, Sing-Min. *Per Capita Consumption Level of Basic Food in Taiwan.* Taiwan: Joint Commission on Rural Reconstruction, 1957.

INDEX

Agarwala, A. N., 5*n*, 6*n*

Aggregate input index: 56*n*, 60, 62, 63, 66, 71, 75, 77, 81, 90, 115, 119; economic content of, 60; in relation to output index, 63, 71, 119; components of, 112, 114

Aggregate input productivity, 12, 66, 68, 119

Agricultural development: 9, 125; versus industrial development, 8, 9; of Japan, 11, 53; rate of, 122

Agricultural employment: 13; data on, 39; estimates of, 41; rate of change in, 42, 45, 118

Agricultural improvement: in relation to industrial development, 8; through reallocation of traditional factors, 10; and human agent, 11; programs, 81

Agricultural labor force: size of, 37, 40, 46, 108; participation rate of, 39–40, 41, 45, 118; in Japan, 107

Agricultural population: displaced, 6, 9; defined, 37; data on, 37, 38; adjusted, 39; from household registration record, 39, 46–47; size of, 46; growth of, 47

Agricultural production: long-term changes in, 15, 18, 20; fluctuation in, 28; peak of, 32; and child labor, 40; the importance of women labor to, 41; improvement in, 67; efficiency of, 78

Agricultural productivity, 36, 67

Agricultural research and education: social return to, 12, 106, 115, 121, 122; and agricultural productivity, 12–13; investment in, 106, 120, 124; contribution of, 108; as the underlying factor, 120

Agricultural revolution, 4, 8

Agricultural surplus: in relation to industrialization, 4; importance to economic development, 7; as a precondition, 8

Animal energy, 53, 118

Association: farmers', 81; marketing, 81; irrigation, 81

Balanced-growth: theory of, 5; Lewis's model, 11

Barclay, George W., 42*n*, 47*n*, 80*n*, 81*n*

Big-push theory, 5, 6, 9

Chemical fertilizers. *See* Commercial fertilizers

Chinese-American Joint Commission on Rural Reconstruction, 18, 21, 23, 24*n*, 59

Coefficient of estimation: of farm products retained, 21

Commercial fertilizers: in Japan's agriculture, 11; as working capital input, 12, 56, 57; imports of, 32; in relation to land quality, 48; application and consumption of, 57, 58, 59, 88, 89, 104, 118, 119, 120; allocation of, 58; cost of, 63; price of, 63*n;* importance to crop yield, 87; supply of, 125

Concurrent development, 9, 10, 125. *See also* Parallel development

Conventional input, 13, 73, 100, 103, 114

Correlation coefficient, 88

Crop area: 49–50, 83, 85, 89*n*, 90, 96, 97, 100, 104; as land input, 51, 90, 91, 114, 115, 118

Crop rotation, 99, 104, 120

Crop yield: in Japan, 11; per unit physical land, 83, 85, 86, 100; per unit of crop area, 85, 86, 87, 88, 89, 89*n*, 90, 103, 120, 121; for all farm products, 85

Crude death rate, 80

Demand elasticity, 5, 5*n*

Development priority, 3

Distributed lag, 105, 106, 108, 113, 115

Domestic fertilizers. *See* Farm-produced fertilizers

Draft animals: draft cattle, 53, 118; water buffalo, 53, 118, population of, 55

flexibility of the formula. In other words, by changing the coefficients, the direction and magnitude of the changes in indices can be accomplished.

ACHIEVEMENT OF SIZE MIXES

Exhibit 63 is the continuation of the same principles laid down in the initial exhibit. There the sizes of the product are rated in terms of proportions of direct profit per pound. These are then multiplied by the pounds per case to produce a combination number which is a weighted profit, per pound, per case. In order to simplify this relationship, these are further reduced then to simple ratios.

EXHIBIT 63   Sales Incentive Calculations

Size Mix

	Profit/Pound	Pounds/Case	×	Reduce
24/2	2.0	3	= 6.0	2.0
24/6	1.6	9	= 14.4	5.0
12/10	0.8	7.5	= 6.0	2.0

District Quota

24/2	5,000	× 2	=	10,000 points
24/6	20,000	× 5	=	100,000 points
12/10	25,000	× 2	=	50,000 points
				160,000 points

Size Mix Adjustment Index

			Subgroups		
Target Achieved	1	2	3	4	5
1	100	60	47	40	36
2		100	73	60	52
3			100	80	68
4				100	84
5					100

Product monies determined by variable profit rate

Our profit plan, which called for a total of $49 million in revenue for the product, also called for 50,000 cases of the product to be sold. It called for a certain proportion in which the cases were to be sold and this proportion is multiplied again by the pounds per case. This multiplication is then transposed into points or more properly, points/pounds. The aggregate points, based upon the size mix called for by the profit plan is 160,000 points in the example shown in Exhibit 63. The purpose of the point evaluation is to permit an area of flexibility to be built into the plan. It is possible at this point to introduce criteria which shall determine whether a district quota has been met or not for purposes of the plan. The reader here is free to introduce any percentage that he chooses; however, as an example, one might say that if 80% of the points are achieved, then this shall constitute full performance, or 100% of the size mix plan required. Upon the satisfaction of the district quota requirements, the size mix adjustment index shown immediately following in Exhibit 63 can be applied. The subgroups shown in the vertical columns indicate the number of mixes or sizes applicable to the product. In the particular case at hand, we would be dealing with subgroup number 3, since there are three sizes to the product.

The left-hand table indicates the number of size goals that were achieved. Thus, if three targets were achieved for three subgroups, or sizes, then 100% of the payout is in order. If, for purposes of example, only 2 out of the 3 size targets were achieved, then 73% would be an adjustment index to be applied to the factor in the initial grid showing revenues and controllable expenses. Therefore, if only 2 out of the 3 sizes were satisfied, although total revenues were achieved in line with controllable expenses, the 100 shown as the index for complete achievement would be multiplied by the size mix adjustment index in 73, to give a final total of 73. That index of 73 would be multiplied by the normative incentive amount of $420 ($1050 − $630). This would result in a payout of $306.60 under this example.

A salesman who qualifies for 100% of individual attributes and who achieved the sales goal of $49 million of revenue, with $9 million of controllable expenses, would be entitled to receive $936.60 under the plan *if* his goal is achieved by satisfying 2 out of the 3 size requirements.

The reader should accept this plan as being far from definitive. It is constructed essentially on sound principles, based upon profitability characteristics of the product and an awareness that qualitative factors are perhaps even more important than those normally associated with volume attainment. Construction of the plan lends itself easily to computer application and to variations in its performance grid.

SEQUENTIAL STEPS FOR SOLUTION

The steps in sequential order for computing this 40% ($420) of the plan, are as follows.

1. Each size of the product should be assigned a point value based on a profitability scale (related to direct profit).

2. Compute total planned point values based on district volume/mix goals.

3. Determine from management the amount of profit it is willing to return to the sales force for each of the following levels of performance:

    (a) 20% below plan

    (b) 10% below plan

    (c) Plan

    (d) 10% above plan

    (e) 20% above plan

4. Based on (3) above, determine the appropriate scaling for expenses and points and apply to chart (Exhibit 62).

5. Compute earned points by multiplying cases for each size by points per case.

6. Apply appropriate product mix adjustment index.

A SIMPLE SHORT FORM PLAN

It is possible to distill concepts contained in the model incentive plan just shown into a somewhat simpler plan. The skeleton plan would be based on profitability concepts outlined in Chapters 2 and 3. For the sake of sim-plicity, products contained in the example shown have been split into four various groups. The groupings are based on the *range* of variable profit less promotional characteristics for the products contained within the group.

Variable profit, the reader may recall, is the amount of incremental profit which accrues as the result of volume. From the marketing side, promotions are a vehicle used to induce a turnover of volume. Therefore, the variable profit, less promotions, in effect, creates a net/net return measure to the company. The range of variable profit, less promotion percentages for each group is as follows.

Group	Variable Profit Less Promotion Percentage Range
1	0 –21.6
2	21.7 –36.0
3	36.1 –50.4
4	50.4 +

The products fall into the groups indicated below:

Group 1	Group 2	Group 3	Group 4
A	C	L	S
B	D	M	T
	E	N	
	F	O	
	G	P	
	H	Q	
	I	R	
	J		
	K		

Once these groups are agreed upon, it is a simple matter to assign a factor to each group (undoubtedly, this factor would be "1" for Group 1, "2" for Group 2, etc.). The increased dollar volume in each district would be multiplied by the appropriate factor to arrive at the number of points which would be used in determining the share of the total "pool" that each district would receive. The total "pool" would contain 5% of the annual increase of direct profit in the division.

The following tabulation gives a hypothetical example of how such a system might work.

Point Calculation		Year 1	Year 2	Incre-mental	Product	
District	Product	Sales	Sales	Sales	Factor	Points
A	L	$100,000	$150,000	$ 50,000	3	150,000
	B	30,000	40,000	10,000	1	10,000
	Total District A			$ 60,000		160,000
B	L	$100,000	$110,000	$ 10,000	3	30,000
	B	30,000	80,000	50,000	1	50,000
	Total District B			$ 60,000		80,000
	Total division points (Districts A and B)					240,000

Total pool calculation
Total division direct profit 2 $5,000,000
Total division direct profit 1   4,500,000
    Annual increase $ 500,000 × 5% = $25,000

Value of each point
Total amount in pool $25,000
Total of points   240,000
Value of each point ($25,000 ÷ 240,000) = $0.10417

Distribution of pool

District	Number of Points	Value of 1 Point	Amount to be Split in District
A	160,000	$0.10417	$16,667
B	80,000	0.10417	8,333
Total division			$25,000

As can be seen from the above tabulation, both District A and District B had an increase in sales of $60,000. However, due to the fact that District A's increase was mostly in product L (which has a factor of 3), rather than product B (factor of 1), District A ended up with a much larger share of the pool than District B. This is quite understandable since product L is far more profitable than product B and should be emphasized.

SUMMARY

The creation of an incentive plan is an art in which the creator assumes the guise of a juggler constantly keeping a multitude of considerations in the air, attempting to be consistent and fair at the same time. Frequently, this is a practical impossibility. Consideration of some of the criteria applications for incentive planning just discussed should go far towards assisting those executives responsible for incentive plans to instill more meaning and fairness into such plans and, at the same time, increase the profitability return to the company.

CHAPTER | 11

Summary

The purpose of a summary chapter is to pull together the content that precedes. I cannot stress strongly enough that the underlying theme of all the material in this book is the use of creativity and sound logic in applying the concept of profitability.

The book has attempted to focus on the processes of control and decision-making which exist under the broad concept of marketing which views the financial area as an ancillary service to marketing function. Of course, under this broad view, other areas such as manufacturing, purchasing, and operations are also looked upon in the same perspective.

One of the realistic challenges posed by the book lies in the area of personnel selection and training. Carried to the extreme, for example, the quest for the proper individual to fill the spot of a marketing controller could result in a search for a man who is faster than a speeding bullet, able to leap small buildings in a single bound, and is more powerful than a speeding locomotive. The essence of a successful term in this position will require that *evolution* and not *revolution* be the guiding principle because the position lies directly between two areas of potentially conflicting views, that is, the conservatism of finance and the optimism of marketing.

I have found that the best means to implement a marketing controller concept within a firm is to recruit mature financial analysts who are familiar with the elements of product, customer, and geographic profitability. In many instances these individuals have had to be "unlearned" from their previous practice of analytical techniques. After a suitable indoctrination period in the use of relevant costing and return on investment techniques, the men were assigned to various marketing vice-presidents to act as *de facto* alter egos. Since their assignments and offices are in the functional marketing area, it has been easy for the individuals to be accepted as participating team members. This type of quiet penetration and friendly persuasion has immeasurably improved the quality of decision making.

In other specific areas, such as *relevant costing* and marketing use of the *return on investment* concept, the utility of these approaches is quite evident. Often, because of accounting, certain marketing options are obscured from being considered as a marketing expense. An example of this occurs when trade terms for extended dating may be changed. Under this type of arrangement a retailer may purchase merchandise and be billed for it as much as six months after the shipping date. It is another promotional tool widely used in the giant food processing industry and sometimes in cosmetics. The extension of the period for payment results in a deprivation of the receipt of money from sales beyond the normal trade term date. Under most practices, such an arrangement results in recording the interest cost of that arrangement under the general heading of "interest" in the operating statement. Under the *relevant* approach such interest cost which is created by virtue of the instituting of specific trade terms would be applied against the product and identified as such. In that manner, the economics of its use as a marketable tool would become quite apparent. Moreover, it facilitates a "what have we received for what we've given?" comparison in that incremental revenues and profits generated by the technique can be measured against their cost of acquisition.

The idea of using *return on investment* as a base against which to measure efficiency and profitability slides by too easily in current business practice. When industry was cited by the government in those instances when price increases were instituted (steels, autos), the direction of the attack was against stable or higher profit margins on the part of the companies. It was not an argument against the declining returns on investment. The measure of this probably comes about from the preoccupation of Americans with profit and loss statements. The balance sheet suffers from relative neglect. There seems to be little regard for the amount of resources which is required to support profits. This observation, though, should not preclude companies from maximizing their utilization of the concept. It has no peer as a decision tool for helping to allocate resources to projects and products.

The concept of *product life cycles* is widely accepted as a general model for forecasting trends in sales of new products and as a basis for planning marketing strategies. If the life cycle is a valid model of sales trends and, if it is equally true that pricing and promotional strategies tend to change as a product passes from one stage of the cycle to the next, then the concept can be useful to the creative marketing executive and also to analysts who are concerned with explaining general patterns of competitive behavior. Most authorities have applied life cycles to new product applications. Nevertheless, there has been surprisingly little study of the actual pattern of sales growth and competition for specific established products and virtually no effective utilization of this widely theorized concept in terms of business reality.

In June 1966, a study establishing the numerical validity of the product life cycle model was made by Dr. Robert D. Buzzell of the Graduate School of Business Administration, Harvard University. The research was supported by the Grocery Manufacturers of America as part of a broad research program for submission to the National Commission of Food Marketing. Subsequently, the research has been continued with the support of the Division of Research, Harvard Business School. This was the first published attempt to establish the quantitative bases of the concept and the findings of the study did, indeed, conform to the product life cycle model. However, the study fell short of suggesting any technique for effective utilization of the concept as a vehicle for planning market strategies.

Beyond the areas specifically touched in this book lies a myriad of other challenges to better decision-making. Mastering of the logic presented here should prove to be a useful base for extending the efficiency of decision-making through the employment of various *decision models*.

Innovation carries with it the potential for a high actuarial risk. It is almost inevitable that this risk be so high since, in many cases, it is difficult to assess technical feasibility, development costs, or exact market potential. Failure beyond the concept and screening stages can probably be avoided or mitigated by more objective analysis and systemization of the enormous quantities of information which are created by present data processing systems.

The construction of models for decision-making is being carried on by various types of organizations. My own research conducted a year ago indicated that few manufacturers were enthusiastic about decision-making models and, indeed, more than one spokesman considered them as fads. Certain specialized companies, however, are making great use of their special models. I am particularly referring to the advertising agencies who control and influence the greater part of the $19 billion national expenditure for this type of marketing investment. They have created decision models with such acronyms as Demon and Sprinter and, moreover, are proving to the business world that the models are truly practical innovations.

The weakness in model usage is in the ability of the human mind and heart to emotionally accept and understand its place in the modern environment. I have no doubt that the use of models will continue to increase and that decision efficiency will be enhanced.

Somewhat philosophically I must state that this work is the culmination of thoughts which occur to me at odd hours. I am certain that most businessmen share with me the experience of receiving the spark of an idea at 2:00 a.m. when everything is quiet or while shaving in the morning. Creativity is a process of impulse and I sincerely hope that you have received some triggering of ideas by reading from, what has been for me, a labor of pure delight.

Index

DATE DUE

NOV. 1 1 1988	NOV 10 '93		
GAYLORD			PRINTED IN U.S.A.